The
Water's Bounty
Member Fish Recipes

North American Fishing Club

The Water's Bounty

Member Fish Recipes

Credits

The Water's Bounty
Member Fish Recipes

Copyright © 2001 North American Fishing Club

Tom Carpenter
Director of Book Development

Julie Cisler
Art Director

Shari Gross
Production Designer

Dan Kennedy
Book Production Manager

Michele Teigen
Senior Book Development Coordinator

Bill Lindner
Photographer

Peter Cozad, Jason Lund
Photography Assistants

Abby Wyckoff
Food Stylist

Pegi Lee, Kimberly Colburn
Food Styling Assistants

1 2 3 4 5 / 05 04 03 02 01
ISBN 1-58159-112-8

North American Fishing Club
12301 Whitewater Drive
Minnetonka, Minnesota 55343
www.fishingclub.com

The North American Fishing club proudly presents this special cookbook edition which includes the personal favorites of your fellow Members. Each recipe has been screened by a cooking professional and edited for clarity. However, we are not able to kitchen-test these recipes and cannot guarantee their outcome, or your safety in their preparation or consumption. Please be advised that any recipes which require the use of dangerous equipment (such as pressure cookers) or potentially unsafe preparation procedures (such as canning and pickling) should be used with caution and safe, healthy practices.

Contents

Introduction

We're all fishing for something. Fortunately, the water offers up many worthwhile bounties.

Escape. Of course, "getting away" is a big part of fishing's allure. Working hard for a living, bearing many responsibilities beyond that … just being on the water, away from everything, can be therapeutic in itself.

People. As a good friend once put it, "just fishin' and conversatin'" is good. It's about sharing a boat or river bend or lakeshore and forgetting for awhile about the challenges of job or school, the commitments of mortgage or vehicle payments, and the necessities of grocery shopping, home maintenance, mowing the lawn and everything else that fills up a life. It's about having some time—with friends or kids or someone you just like—to talk about things that do (and pleasantly enough, *don't*) matter.

Places. The places you go, to go fishing, matter too. Maybe it's a bass pond near home. A panfish or pickerel-filled lake down the road. A sprawling reservoir halfway across the state. A clear trout stream you love. A salty breakwater or pier. A charter boat out on the big water. A cabin or resort you dream of often. A murky, catfish river only you could love. Pristine or not, these places draw us.

Fish! Absolutely—catching fish is a necessary part of the water's bounty and allure. Yes it's true that just getting away from everyday life matters. But no matter how beautiful the place or how good the company, I for one want to at least have the chance of catching some fish.

In this day and age of catch-and-release ethics, it's a good bet that once you get that fish in your hands you are going to put him or her back. And that's great. We recite all the reasons as we slip the fish back: "Go back so I can catch you again. Live to breed another day. It took a long time to grow you—it's not fair to just kill you and call it good."

Meals. Yet the water produces still another bounty: great fish meals. Yes, not every fish need go back. Where regulations per-mit and you're not hurting the resource, there's nothing wrong with saving a few fish to eat. It's truly another bounty, and it's the one around which we chose to create this book.

We went to one of the most reliable sources we know—North American Fishing Club members—to find the recipes that follow. And we received ideas by the hundreds. Thinking about the quality of what we saw, it is clear that your and my fellow members know how to cook fish *right*!

It's not easy to make a book like this. We always receive more recipes than can fit on the allotted pages. Whittling down is hard for both the whittler and the whittled. But every minute of labor seems well spent when the final product is in hand. It's then that you realize everybody who sent in a recipe, whether it's printed here or not, helped create this book. Thank you.

So take some time to appreciate all the bounty the water has to offer—escape, people, places, fish … and great meals. *The Water's Bounty— Member Fish Recipes* is here to help you make the most of that last reward. Now it's up to you to get out there—just go fishin'— and enjoy *all* the bounty the water has to offer.

Tom

Tom Carpenter
Editor—North American
Fishing Club Books

Jim's Fish Grill, Page 38

Just Fish

Sometimes it seems that you dare not go out after one species of fish without boat, electronics, rods, reels, lines, terminal tackle, baits (and more!) geared only to that fish. Yes, it can be hard to remember that fishing can also be done for the sheer joy of it, for whatever's biting. Recipes are the same way. Specialized ideas calling for one type of fish are fine. But it's also good to have recipes that are just for fish—any fish—the fish that bit that day and you decided to bring home or to camp.

Cranberry Glazed Fish Steaks,
Page 43

9

Fish Gumbo Filé

Fish Gumbo Filé

1 T. bacon drippings
1 bunch green onions, chopped
1 cup diced tomatoes
6 cups soup stock or chicken bouillon
1 red bell pepper, diced
1 green bell pepper, diced
1 cup diced celery
½ tsp. thyme
1 bay leaf
Salt, to taste
1 lb. fish, diced
1 T. filé powder

In large saucepan, heat bacon drippings; sauté onions. Add tomatoes; cook 5 minutes. Add stock, peppers, celery, thyme, bay leaf and salt. Heat to boiling; add fish. Stir in filé; serve.

Daniel Tomlinson
Dallas, Texas

A Fast & Easy Fish Fry

Walleye or bass fillet
Salt water
Flour
1 egg, beaten
Cornmeal
Vegetable oil

Soak fish in salt water. Rub fish on a plate of flour. Dip fish in egg and then rub fish on a plate of cornmeal. The egg acts like a paste. Heat oil in skillet. Cook fillet in oil until slightly browned. Cooking time depends on fillet size.

Greg Haut
Waukesha, Wisconsin

Batter-Fried Fish

1 gallon vanilla ice cream mix (commercial style)
Flour
Cornmeal
White pepper, to taste
Salt, to taste
Fish fillets (channel cat, black bass, striper, crappie)

Place ice cream in large bowl. Make mixture of one part flour to two parts cornmeal. Add white pepper and salt. Soak fish in ice cream mix for about 30 minutes in refrigerator. Dip fish in cornmeal mix and fry until golden brown.

Steve Carr
Peoria, Arizona

Fish Quesadillas with Green Salsa

Quesadillas
2 garlic cloves, chopped
1 medium onion, chopped
4 tomatoes, chopped
2 bay leaves
1 lb. white meat fish fillet, chopped
½ tsp. oregano
½ tsp. salt
2 medium chile peppers, chopped
10 corn tortillas
2 T. vegetable oil

Green Salsa
½ lb. tomatillos
2 small chiles
¼ cup cilantro leaves
½ small onion, minced
½ tsp. salt

Fish Quesadillas:
Sauté garlic and onion in skillet for 30 seconds on medium heat. Add tomatoes, bay leaves, fish, oregano, salt and chile peppers. Cook for 10 to 15 minutes on medium heat. Check fish for doneness. Warm tortillas and stuff with fish mixture by folding tortilla in half. Hold together with toothpicks. Fry tortillas in vegetable oil until crisp. Serve with green salsa (see recipe below).

Green Salsa:
Heat broiler or grill. Place tomatillos and chiles in baking pan; cook until lightly brown and soft. Set aside when done. Pulse tomatillos, chiles and cilantro leaves in blender. Place in serving bowl. Stir in onion and season with salt.

Richard Gunion
Washington, D.C.

Fish & Shrimp Chowder

1 cup diced red new potatoes
1½ qts. fish stock
2 strips bacon, diced
3 oz. butter
1 small onion, diced
2 or 3 ribs celery, diced
4 oz. flour
2 cups heavy cream or half-and-half
1 cup chopped clams in juice or
   bouillon cubes in hot water
1 cup shrimp
½ cup corn kernels
½ cup chopped fresh tomatoes
1 lb. walleye fillets, cut into bite-
   size chunks
2 T. chopped parsley
1 tsp. chopped thyme
Salt, to taste
Pepper, to taste

Cover potatoes with fish stock in large Dutch oven; simmer until potatoes are done. In separate skillet, fry bacon until partially rendered. Add butter, onion and celery; sauté until onions are translucent. Add flour; combine with wire whisk to make a roux. Cook 5 to 6 minutes, stirring constantly. Add hot fish stock gradually, stirring until thick and smooth. Add cream and clams in juice; simmer 10 minutes. Stir in shrimp, corn and tomatoes gently. Add walleye chunks, parsley, thyme, salt and pepper; simmer 3 to 4 minutes or until fish is done.

Mike Vondrak
Newport, Michigan

Fish Quesadillas with Green Salsa

Fish Curry

2 lbs. fish
1 ½ tsp. salt
¼ tsp. turmeric
½ tsp. garlic powder
2 tsp. lemon juice
1 large onion, chopped
3 T. cooking oil
1 tsp. ginger
¼ tsp. cayenne pepper
1 tsp. curry powder
1 can tomato sauce
2 cups water

Cut fish into 2-inch pieces. Mix 1 teaspoon salt with ⅛ teaspoon turmeric and ¼ teaspoon garlic powder. Lightly rub salt mixture on all fish pieces, sprinkle with lemon juice and set aside for 30 minutes. Sauté onion in oil until golden brown. Add rest of turmeric and garlic powder, along with ginger, cayenne pepper and curry. Stir for 30 seconds; add tomato sauce. Cover pan and cook over low heat for 7 minutes, stirring occasionally. Add water and remaining salt. Bring to a boil, add fish pieces, cover and simmer over low heat until done. Serve with cooked rice.

Mary Houchin
Swansea, Illinois

Batter-Fried Fish Fillets

Vegetable oil
1 cup flat beer (beat with fork to
    lose carbonation)
Bannock mix (see recipe below)
Salt, to taste
Pepper, to taste
Flour
Fish fillets or fish pieces

Bannock Mix
1 cup flour
¼ cup dry milk powder
1 tsp. baking powder
¼ tsp. salt
1 T. shortening

Add enough oil to cast-iron skillet and preheat to 350°F. Add flat beer to Bannock mix and beat to pancake batter consistency. Add salt and pepper to flour and coat fish with mixture. Dip fish into batter and fry one or two pieces at a time in preheated oil. Fish will float when done.

Bannock Mix:
Sift dry ingredients. Mix into shortening until whole package is granular.

John Pelrine
Chicago, Illinois

Campfire Fish Chowder

3 (15-oz.) cans creamed corn
2 (15-oz.) cans potatoes, cooked,
    sliced
1 cup chopped green onion
¼ cup minced green pepper
4 (5 oz.) fish fillets, cooked and
    diced
Salt, to taste
Pepper, to taste
1 tsp. garlic powder (optional)

Pour corn, potatoes, green onion, green pepper, fish, salt, pepper and garlic into cast-iron skillet; cook over campfire or campstove for 30 minutes.

Jennifer Ann Kunze
Grand Rapids, Minnesota

Fish Curry

Whitefish Amandine

2 lbs. whitefish fillets
2 T. lemon juice
2 tsp. salt
Dash of pepper
½ cup flour
½ cup oil
½ cup slivered blanched almonds
2 T. chopped parsley

Cut whitefish into serving-size pieces. Sprinkle with lemon juice, salt and pepper. Coat with flour. Brown both sides of fish in oil in skillet over medium heat. Cook for 10 to 12 minutes or until tender. Remove whitefish to hot platter. Sauté almonds until lightly browned. Add parsley. Spoon over whitefish. Makes 6 servings.

Ryan Wilson
Cypress, Texas

Fish Boil

¼ cup salt
10 to 12 new, red potatoes, ends cut off
1 large white onion, chopped
1½ to 2 lbs. fish (cod, perch, crappie, bass, bluegill), cut into 1-inch chunks

Fill large saucepan with water (about 1 gallon) and ⅛ cup of salt. Bring to a boil. Add potatoes; boil for 20 minutes. Add onion; continue to boil for 5 minutes. Add fish chunks and remaining salt; boil for another 10 to 15 minutes or until fish are done. Drain and serve with butter.

Dale Galbreath
Morris, Illinois

Boiling Recipe

3½ to 4 lb. fish (whitefish, shellfish, pike, cod, bass, flounder, sole, carp, salmon, trout, brook trout, etc.)
4 qts. water
Salt, to taste
4 cloves
1 large onion
2 bay leaves
10 peppercorns

Dress and wash fish. Pour water into large saucepan. Add remaining ingredients to water—make sure to add enough salt to make it quite salty. Place fish on tray of pot in a swimming position and bring slowly to a boil; boil 5 minutes. Then set back to draw ½ hour. When the meat near gills is not bloody anymore, fish is done. Rinse with hot water before serving. Garnish with lemon slices, parsley, lettuce and potatoes.

Note: you can also serve this with a fish gravy, mustard gravy or béarnaise gravy, or fresh creamed butter, browned butter, mustard butter or parsley butter.

Sean Cunningham
Taylor, Texas

Mary's Special Fish

4 to 6 fish fillets
Salt, to taste
Pepper, to taste
Garlic powder or cloves, to taste
1 to 2 bay leaves
1 can tomato sauce
1 tomato, sliced
1 small green pepper, sliced
1 onion, sliced

Cook fish and spices in just enough water to cover fish, about 10 minutes. Add rest of ingredients, cover and simmer until vegetables are tender. May be served with rice.

Mary Houchin
Swansea, Illinois

Fish Cakes

4 medium potatoes
2 cups shredded, cooked fish
1 small onion, minced
Salt, to taste
Pepper, to taste
¼ tsp. curry powder (optional)
3 eggs
1 cup dry bread or cracker crumbs
½ cup butter

Boil potatoes; put through ricer (or very finely chopped). Combine fish, potatoes, onion, salt, pepper and curry; stir in eggs. Shape into cakes and dip into crumbs. Sauté in butter until brown. The butter should be hot as for any other kind of fat frying. If a food grinder is available, run the fish, potatoes and onion through it, rather than preparing them separately. When cakes are nicely browned, drain them on absorbent paper towels. They can be served with tomato sauce, ketchup or tartar sauce.

Luke Moeller
Downers Grove, Illinois

Bacon-Fried Fish

4 to 6 lbs. white fish
2 lbs. bacon
6 whole eggs
2 lbs. Bisquick
1 loaf French bread
Salt, to taste
Pepper, to taste

Fillet fish; remove skin. Fry bacon in cast-iron skillet. Scramble eggs in bowl. When bacon is crispy, remove and set on covered plate. Leave bacon fat in skillet. Dip fish fillets in eggs; then dredge in Bisquick, coating both sides of fillets. Place in skillet. Cook both sides evenly. When fish is done, flesh will flake easily with a fork. Serve bacon and fish together with bread. Season with salt and pepper.

Greg Martin
Orlando, Florida

Fish Roll

1 can crescent rolls
1½ cups flaked, cooked fish
1 small onion, chopped
1 green pepper, chopped
½ tsp. salt
Milk

On floured board, roll crescent dough to ¼-inch thickness. Combine fish, onion, green pepper and salt. Moisten slightly with milk. Mix well and spread mixture on dough. Roll as for jelly roll and cut into 1½-inch slices. Bake on greased baking sheet in 400°F oven for 30 minutes.

Bob Rhoads
Mount Vernon, Indiana

Fish Cakes

2 lbs. fish fillets
Salt, to taste
1 lb. mashed potatoes
4 T. finely chopped onion
4 tsp. chopped parsley
8 tsp. anchovy essence
Pepper, to taste
4 eggs
Flour
2 oz. cooking oil

Boil fish in salted water. Drain and flake fish. Thoroughly mix fish, mashed potatoes, onion, parsley, anchovy essence, pepper and eggs. Shape into patties; roll in flour. Fry in skillet of hot, shallow oil until brown.

Mary Houchin
Swansea, Illinois

Vonnita's Fish Cakes

1 lb. fish fillets (crappie or catfish)
1 egg
¼ cup chopped green pepper
½ cup chopped green onion
¼ cup mayonnaise
1 T. Dijon mustard
Salt, to taste
Pepper, to taste
2 T. bread crumbs (or more)
1 cup flour (for dredging)
1 tsp. curry powder

Finely chop fish. Mix fish, egg, green pepper, onion, mayonnaise, mustard, salt, pepper and bread crumbs. Refrigerate 30 minutes or more. Mix flour and curry. Form fish mixture into patties and dredge in flour mixture. Heat butter in heavy skillet on medium heat. Fry patties until browned. Serve with lemon wedges and tartar sauce.

Vonnita Collins
Joelton, Tennessee

Fish Roll

Baked Fish

3 ½ to 4 lbs. fish
Salt, to taste
Flour
¼ lb. butter
1½ cups sour or sweet cream
¼ tsp. meat extract
Juice of ½ lemon
1 T. Parmesan cheese
1 T. capers
3 peppercorns

Wash and dry fish. Salt inside and outside; roll in flour. Melt butter; pour in porcelain dish. Place fish in dish. Put in oven and bake for 10 minutes or until fish is a light yellow color. Baste with the cream, meat extract and lemon juice. Sprinkle on cheese, and add capers and peppercorns. Stew it ½ hour.

Sean Cunningham
Taylor, Texas

Fish Fillets Florentine

3 lbs. spinach, canned or fresh
¼ cup butter
1½ T. flour
½ tsp. salt
⅛ tsp. pepper
1½ cups milk
½ cup grated cheese
2 lbs. fish fillets

Wash spinach several times, or use canned spinach. Drain and coarsely chop. Place in baking dish. Melt butter; blend in flour, salt and pepper. Add milk and cook until thickened, stirring constantly. Add cheese and continue heating until cheese has melted. Pour sauce over spinach, place fillets on top and bake in 375°F oven for about 30 minutes.

Hanne Anderson
Council, Idaho

Baked Fish

1 cup crushed potato chips
1 tsp. parsley flakes
1 lb. fish fillets
¼ cup milk
1 T. oleo, melted
Salt, to taste
Pepper, to taste

Mix chips and parsley. Dip fish in milk, then in chips. Layer in greased 8 x 6 x 2-inch baking dish. Place extra crumbs of chips on top and pour melted oleo over top. Salt and pepper to taste. Cover with foil and bake 30 to 40 minutes at 350°F.

Kenneth Finch
Minot, Maine

Baked Fish with Tarragon

1 egg
½ cup milk
1 lb. fish fillets
¼ lb. crushed soda crackers
1 cup white sauce (see recipe below)
1 tsp. tarragon
Oleo

White Sauce
3 T. oleo
3 T. flour
¼ tsp. salt
Dash of pepper
1 cup milk

Fish:
Mix egg and milk. Dip fillets in mixture; roll in cracker crumbs. Layer fillets in greased 9 x 13-inch pan. Pour white sauce over fillets. Evenly sprinkle tarragon over fillets. Add cracker crumbs (no more than ½ cup) and any remaining egg and milk. Dot top with oleo and bake at 350°F for 30 to 40 minutes.

White Sauce:
Heat oleo in saucepan until melted and bubbly. Combine flour and seasonings; gradually add to oleo. Gradually add milk, while stirring. Boil for 2 minutes.

Kenneth Finch
Minot, Maine

Zesty Baked Fish

½ cup mayonnaise
2 T. lemon juice
2 T. Worcestershire sauce
1 tsp. paprika
2 tsp. chopped parsley
½ cup cheese
2 T. butter
1 onion, sliced
Fish
Oregano, to taste

Heat mayonnaise, lemon juice, Worcestershire sauce, paprika, parsley and cheese until cheese melts. Melt butter in baking pan or dish. Cover butter with sliced onion. Place fish on onions. Pour cheese sauce over fish. Sprinkle well with oregano. Bake uncovered in 375°F oven for 30 minutes.

Note: If you are camping, you will need a camp oven for this dish. You could try making this in several layers of heavy-duty aluminum foil over medium-hot coals or in a Dutch oven.

Mary Houchin
Swansea, Illinois

Beer-Batter Fish

1 lb. fish fillets
1½ cups unsifted flour
2¼ tsp. baking powder
½ tsp. baking soda
1½ tsp. salt
⅓ cup lemon juice
⅔ cup beer
1 cup vegetable oil

Place fish on paper towels; pat dry. Mix together flour, baking powder, baking soda and salt. Coat fish with ½ cup mix. In large bowl, combine the remaining dry mixture with lemon juice and beer. This will foam. Stir until pancake batter consistency. In large skillet, heat oil over medium heat. Dip fish into batter, fry until golden brown on both sides. Drain on paper towels. We have used this recipe on freshwater and saltwater fish fillets.

George Bragg
Rochester, New Hampshire

White Fish with Tomato & Orange Sauce

White Fish with Tomato & Orange Sauce

3 T. flour
Salt, to taste
Pepper, to taste
4 firm white fish fillets
1 T. butter
2 T. olive oil
1 onion, sliced
1 oz. fresh garlic, chopped
¼ tsp. ground cumin
1¼ lbs. tomatoes, skinned, seeded
   and chopped or 1 (14-oz.) can
   chopped tomatoes
½ cup fresh orange juice

Put flour on plate; season well with salt and pepper. Coat fish fillets lightly with seasoned flour; shake off excess. Heat butter and 1 tablespoon of oil in skillet. Add fish to pan; cook for 3 minutes on each side, or until golden brown and the flesh flakes easily. When fish is cooked, transfer to warmed serving platter. Cover with foil; keep warm until the sauce is made. Heat remaining oil in skillet. Add onion and garlic; cook for 5 minutes until softened, but not colored. Stir in ground cumin, tomatoes and orange juice. Bring to a boil and cook, stirring frequently, for 10 minutes until thickened. Serve fish and sauce separately.

Greg Martin
Orlando, Florida

Ken's Krispy Baked Fish

2 T. oil
1 lb. fish fillets
½ cup crushed corn flakes
½ tsp. salt
¼ tsp. pepper

Place oil in 9 x 13-inch baking dish. Wash and dry fish; cut into serving-size pieces. Place fish in dish. Turn over until lightly oiled on both sides. Put corn flakes, salt and pepper in plastic bag and shake well. Put fish in bag with flakes and shake until well coated. Place fish in baking dish; bake for 10 minutes at 500°F. Do not baste or turn.

Kenneth Finch
Minot, Maine

Baked Fish Fillets

1 lb. fish fillets
½ tsp. pepper
½ can mushroom soup
¼ cup milk
¼ tsp. salt
¼ tsp. onion salt
1 T. dried parsley flakes
2 T. butter

Cut fish into 5 or 6 serving-size pieces; arrange in baking dish. Combine pepper, soup, milk, salt and onion salt. Pour around fish. Sprinkle with additional pepper and parsley flakes. Dot with butter. Bake at 350°F for 20 to 25 minutes or until fish flakes easily.

Ryan Wilson
Cypress, Texas

Baked Fish in Foil

2 lbs. fish fillets
2 T. oil or nonstick spray
12 chopped scallions, cut into 6
  equal parts
2 tomatoes, chopped
2 small zucchini, thinly sliced
½ tsp. salt
½ tsp. pepper
1 tsp. dried oregano
Juice of 2 lemons

Preheat oven to 375°F. Cut 6 pieces of aluminum foil large enough to hold ⅙ of the fish. Brush fish with oil or spray with nonstick cooking spray. Place fish in center of foil and top with ⅙ of the vegetables on each piece. Sprinkle with salt, pepper, oregano and some lemon juice. Wrap into 6 packages; bake on cookie sheet for 20 minutes.

Kenneth Finch
Minot, Maine

Easy Fried Fish

1 egg
1 tsp. salt
1 tsp. pepper
1 cup yellow cornmeal
2 lbs. fish fillets
Oil

In small bowl, beat egg; add salt and pepper. Put cornmeal in separate bowl. When ready to fix fish, dip fillet in egg mixture and then in cornmeal, being sure to coat both sides evenly with both ingredients. Fry in oil until golden brown.

Damon Black
Boise, Idaho

Parmesan Breaded Fish

⅓ cup milk
1 egg, beaten
½ cup bread crumbs
⅓ cup grated Parmesan or Romano
  cheese
White fish fillets (flounder, bass,
  trout, catfish, etc.)
  Fresh lemon (optional)

Combine milk and egg in shallow bowl. In separate bowl, combine bread crumbs and grated cheese. After washing each fillet, pat dry. Dip both sides of fillet in the bread crumb mixture. Dip both sides in milk and egg mixture, followed by another round in the bread crumbs. You may fry or bake fish.

For frying:
Preheat skillet on medium heat and cover bottom of pan with light vegetable oil or olive oil. Cook breaded fillets on both sides until brown. Serve immediately with couscous or rice and your favorite vegetable. Add freshly squeezed lemon for a nice touch.

For baking:
Preheat oven to 400°F. Place breaded fillets on shallow baking sheet. Squeeze juice from fresh lemon on fillets and cook until fish is done. Thin fillets like flounder or trout may take 10 to 15 minutes. Thicker fillets will cook longer. Serve immediately with couscous or baked potato, along with your favorite vegetable.

Ken Lefkowitz
Basking Ridge, New Jersey

Fish Fillets in Sauce

5 T. butter or margarine
2 T. flour
1 cup milk
1 cube chicken bouillon
1 tsp. lemon juice
1 bay leaf
2 T. finely chopped onion,
1 lb. fish fillets
½ cup fine bread crumbs

Melt 2 tablespoons butter in saucepan. Stir in flour; let simmer for 1 minute. Add milk, bouillon cube, lemon juice and bay leaf. Cook over medium heat until thickened. In separate pan, sauté onion in remaining butter until tender. Add bread crumbs and combine. Pour sauce over fillets in baking dish. Top with bread crumbs. Bake at 350°F for 35 minutes.

Mrs. Daniel Zell
Crownsville, Maryland

Stuffed Fish Fillet

4 fresh white fish
Salt, to taste
Pepper, to taste
3 T. chopped onion
¼ cup chopped celery
2 T. plus additional butter
1 cup bread crumbs
1 orange
1 T. chopped parsley

Sprinkle fish with salt and pepper. Sauté onion and celery in butter until tender. Add bread crumbs; blend well. Grate 1 teaspoon orange peel. Peel orange; dice slices. Add to mixture, along with parsley, salt and pepper. Place mixture on fish to about ¼ inch thick. Roll fish; secure with toothpick. Brush with additional melted butter and sprinkle with parsley. Bake in ungreased, uncovered dish for about 20 minutes at 350°F.

Dan Benson
Savage, Minnesota

Fish Casserole

1 (10½-oz.) can cream of mushroom
  soup
1 (15-oz.) can mixed vegetables,
  drained
Fish fillets (catfish, bass, crappie,
  perch)
Cheese

Put cream of mushroom soup in casserole dish. Add mixed vegetables. Layer with choice of fish fillets. Top with cheese and bake in oven at 350°F for 30 to 40 minutes.

Garland Lee Zimmerman
Malden, Missouri

Pineapple-Orange Chutney Bake

Pineapple-Orange Chutney Bake

1 (8-oz.) can unsweetened crushed
   pineapple, moderately drained
¼ cup shredded coconut
⅓ cup chopped walnuts
Zest from 1 medium orange
Fish fillets (works best with thicker
   white fillets like codfish, halibut,
   etc.)

Preheat oven to 375°F. Combine pineapple, coconut, walnuts and orange zest in medium bowl. Tear off enough aluminum foil to cover fish. Wash fish and place in center of foil on baking sheet. Cover the fish with pineapple mixture, including liquid, and seal the foil. Bake for 15 to 20 minutes or until done. The fish has a nice sweet flavor and will absorb the chutney.

Ken Lefkowitz
Basking Ridge, New Jersey

Blackened Fish

¼ cup margarine
2 lbs. fish fillets
1 T. paprika
1 tsp. salt
1 tsp. onion powder
1 tsp. garlic powder
1½ tsp. black pepper
½ tsp. cayenne pepper
½ tsp. thyme
½ tsp. oregano

Melt margarine. Dip both sides of fish in margarine. Combine dry ingredients. Sprinkle on both sides of fish; press the spices into fish with your fingers. Place fish in baking dish. Bake until fish is solid white and flakes. Garnish with red cherry peppers, parsley and lemon wedges.

Matthew Sirmans
North Palm Beach, Florida

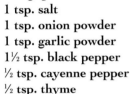

Anglers' Delight

Butter
Salt, to taste
Pepper, to taste
Garlic powder
Onion powder
Mrs. Dash
Seasoned salt
Fish fillets
1 to 2 pkgs. McCormick or
   Durkee's white sauce
Almonds
Paprika
Almonds or cashews, slivered

Preheat oven to 350°F. Melt enough butter to coat bottom of baking dish. Mix in salt, pepper, garlic powder, onion powder, Mrs. Dash original spice and seasoned salt. Add fish to buttered dish and lay flat. Prepare packages of McCormick or Durkee's white sauce; cover fish thoroughly. Bake for 20 to 30 minutes or until fish flakes. Add almond slices or cashews over fish and finish by sprinkling paprika over entire dish.

Note: as you watch it cook, the butter will work its way to the top. When you pull the dish out of the oven, the sauce will return to the top and the butter to the bottom. If you want, you can also add onions and mushrooms with the sauce.

Bruce Kitowski
Saint Joseph, Minnesota

Bob's Baked Fish—Fast but Not Fancy

2 lbs. fish fillets or steaks
1 (10¾-oz.) can condensed soup
Milk
Salt, to taste
Pepper, to taste

Place fish in baking pan. Pour soup in mixing bowl. Mix in a little milk to thin soup. Pour mixture over fish. Sprinkle with salt and pepper. Bake at 400°F for about 30 to 40 minutes (depending on thickness of fish). Any soup can be used according to your taste—tomato, mushroom, cream of broccoli, cheddar cheese, etc.

Robert S. Kukuvka
Rockaway, New Jersey

Fish Goulash

2 lbs. fish fillets
Oil
Cayenne pepper, to taste
10 to 12 green onions, sliced
1 medium yellow onion, sliced
½ cup flour
1 (6-oz.) can green chiles, chopped
4 to 5 garlic cloves, crushed
1 medium green pepper, chopped
1 (12-oz.) can stewed tomatoes
1 cup picante sauce
Salt, to taste
Pepper, to taste

Brown fish fillets in oil, then place in bottom of 6-quart slow cooker. Layer the rest of the ingredients on top of fish. Slow cook on high heat for 4 hours, stirring occasionally. Serve over white or wild rice. Also good served over macaroni noodles.

Dave Walters
Craig, Colorado

Spanish-Style Baked Fillets

2 lbs. fish fillets
2 large tomatoes, thinly sliced
½ medium cucumber, thinly sliced
2½ tsp. butter
⅔ cup chopped onion
½ cup chopped green pepper
1 clove garlic, minced
2½ tsp. parsley
2½ tsp. lemon juice
1 tsp. marjoram

Cut fillets into 6 to 8 serving-size pieces. Place fish in greased baking pan; arrange tomatoes and cucumber slices on top. In saucepan, melt butter and cook onion, green pepper and garlic until onion is tender, but not browned. Remove from heat; stir in parsley, lemon juice and marjoram. Spoon over fillets. Bake in preheated 375°F oven for 25 minutes or until fish flakes easily with fork.

Jim Gallant
Yarmouthport, Massachusetts

Nippy's Own Light & Cheesy Fillets

1 lb. fish fillets
Lemon pepper seasoning, to taste
1 small onion
1 large tomato, diced
Oregano, to taste
Mozzarella cheese

Preheat oven to 375°F. Cut fillets into serving-size pieces. Place fillets in lightly greased baking dish. Season with lemon pepper. Grate onion over fish. Cover with tomato and bake for 15 to 20 minutes or until fish flakes easily with fork. Top with oregano and mozzarella cheese; place in broiler until cheese is fully melted.

Jim Gallant
Yarmouthport, Massachusetts

Baked Fish with Cheese Sauce

2 lbs. fish fillets
¼ tsp. ground black pepper
2 (11-oz.) cans cheddar cheese soup
½ tsp. onion powder
½ cup milk
1 tsp. prepared mustard
3 cups cooked rice
Paprika

Season fillets with pepper; set aside. Combine soup, onion powder, milk and mustard. Spoon rice into greased shallow baking dish. Place fillets on top of rice. Pour sauce over fish; sprinkle with paprika. Bake at 400°F for 20 to 30 minutes or until fish flakes easily with fork. Makes 6 servings.

Jane Hunter
Bullhead City, Arizona

Oven-Fried Fish

5 oz. fish
1½ T. bread crumbs
1 T. olive or cooking oil
Salt, to taste
Pepper, to taste

Dip fish in bread crumbs. Place in baking dish or pan sprayed with non-stick spray. Drizzle oil over fish. Sprinkle with salt and pepper. Bake for 10 to 15 minutes at 500°F (time depends on thickness of fish). Makes 1 serving.

Mary Houchin
Swansea, Illinois

Pasta Puttanesca with Fish

6 cloves garlic, diced
2 medium onions, diced into ½-inch
   pieces
¼ cup vegetable oil
2 (28-oz.) cans diced tomatoes
1 (6-oz.) can tomato paste
½ cup white wine
1 can large pitted black olives,
   crushed
1 small jar green sliced olives
1 T. cayenne pepper
1 T. dillweed
1 T. oregano flakes
3 T. parsley flakes
1 (6-oz.) can anchovies in oil, finely
   diced (drain oil in saucepan)
Salt, to taste
Pepper, to taste
1½ lbs. fish, boneless, skinned, cut
   into ½-inch cubes
2 lbs. linguine

In saucepan, sauté garlic and onions in oil for 3 minutes. Add tomatoes, tomato paste, wine, olives, cayenne, dillweed, oregano, parsley, anchovies, salt and pepper. Bring to low boil, reduce heat to a simmer, add fish and cover. Simmer for 20 minutes. Serve over hot linguine with bread sticks.

Rod Wodzinski
Iron River, Michigan

Mushroom Fish

¼ cup butter
2 T. parsley
¼ cup green onion
1 cup finely chopped mushrooms
2 T. lemon juice
¼ to ½ tsp. dill weed
1½ to 2 lbs. fish fillets
Salt, to taste
Pepper, to taste

Melt butter in small saucepan. Add parsley, green onion, mushrooms, lemon juice and dill; stir until mixed. Spread half the sauce mixture in bottom of microwave dish. Add fillets and pour remaining sauce on top. Sprinkle with salt and pepper. Cover and cook on high for 6 to 8 minutes. Let stand, covered, for 2 minutes. Serve with wild rice and veggie of your choice.

Larry Darling
Athens, Ontario, Canada

Fish Patties

1 pint fish
10 crackers, crushed
¼ tsp. pepper
¼ tsp. salt
¼ cup chopped onion
2 eggs

Combine all ingredients together; make into patties. Fry on low heat for 10 to 15 minutes or until golden brown.

Randall Webb
Fife Lake, Michigan

Pasta Puttanesca with Fish

Fish in Chips

1 (6-oz.) bag potato chips
¼ tsp. ground celery seeds
¼ tsp. dried thyme
2¼ T. unsalted butter
1 lb. fresh white fish fillets, cut into
    8 pieces
Salt, to taste
Pepper, to taste

Place a few handfuls of potato chips in plastic bag. Close bag tightly and put on a work surface. With a rolling pin, crush enough potato chips to fill one cup. Put crushed chips on plate. Add celery seeds and thyme to chips and stir lightly with fork. Preheat oven to 500°F. Put butter in skillet; place on low heat until butter melts. Turn off heat. Brush butter on inside of baking pan. Dip each piece of fish into melted butter. Roll the fish in the chips, patting the chips with your fingers. Place fish in baking pan. Make sure fillets aren't touching. Sprinkle fish with salt and pepper. Drizzle with remaining melted butter. Place pan in oven on center rack. Bake fish until coating is golden brown and fish flakes easily with a fork, 7 to 8 minutes. Do not overcook. Serve immediately.

Joseph Barry
Burbank, Illinois

Stove Top Special

1 box stuffing mix
Carrots, thinly sliced
1 onion, thinly sliced
Lake trout or salmon fillets
Butter or margarine
Salt, to taste
Pepper, to taste
Parsley flakes

On large sheet of aluminum foil, layer half of prepared stuffing. On top of stuffing, layer half of carrots and onion. Place fish fillets on top. Add another layer of carrots, onion and stuffing. Fold and seal foil. Put in Dutch oven. Bake using charcoal briquettes for 20 to 25 minutes. Poke holes in foil for last 5 minutes of cooking. Serve.

John Pelrine
Chicago, Illinois

Campfire Fish

Fish fillets
Pepper, to taste
Lemon, sliced
Yellow onion, sliced
Garlic
3 pats butter

Build fire and let burn to coals. Sprinkle filleted fish with a lot of pepper. Squeeze lemon slice on fish. Lay generous slices of onion, garlic and butter on 1-foot-long piece of aluminum foil. Lay fish on top and repeat process. Cook over hot coals until fish is done.

Steve Carr
Peoria, Arizona

Fish with Veggies

Several potatoes, diced
1 to 2 onions, diced
Nonstick cooking spray
Garlic salt, to taste
Salt, to taste
Pepper, to taste
Fresh tomatoes, sliced
Small zucchini squash, sliced
Fish fillets (catfish, walleye, bass, etc.)
Oil or butter
Seasoned salt

Fire up gas grill on low to medium heat. Place potatoes and onions on aluminum foil sprayed with nonstick cooking spray. Add garlic salt, salt, pepper and any other seasonings you wish. Wrap foil tightly; place on top shelf of gas grill. Wrap tomatoes and zucchini in separate foil, season with garlic salt, salt and pepper, wrap tightly and place on grill also. Let vegetables cook for 20 minutes before putting the fillets on burner. To cook fish, use a cookie sheet on the main cooking area of the grill. Use just enough oil or butter to keep the fillets from sticking. Season fillets with a little seasoned salt. Cook about 10 minutes on each side. Place thin slice of onion on top if you wish.

Rich Hopkins
Valparaiso, Indiana

Down by the River Dinner

4 fresh fish fillets
4 medium Idaho potatoes, sliced ¼ inch thick
4 sheets heavy-duty aluminum foil (each 12 to 14 inches long)
Lemon pepper seasoning
Bacon bits, to taste
2 medium white onions, sliced
1 large green pepper, sliced

Prepare a campfire and clean fish. Place raw potatoes on each foil sheet. Season both sides of fish with lemon pepper and lay flat on top of potatoes. Sprinkle bacon bits directly on fish. Place onions and peppers on top of fish. Seal foil and cook on hot coals for about 45 minutes, turning every 15 minutes.

Note: to add a touch of flair to this simple meal, try leaving the shucks on ears of corn while removing the corn silk. Bring the shucks back up to cover the ear of corn. Soak the corn in water for about an hour prior to fixing the above meal. Place the ears of corn onto the hot coals to cook along with the fish. As you turn the fish, turn the corn. Cook for the same amount of time. Peel back the shucks and enjoy a very tasty ear of corn!

Odell Underwood
Mount Hope, West Virginia

Here Fishy, Fishy, Fishy Shore Lunch

2 cans homestyle baked beans with onions
1 pkg. dry buttermilk salad dressing
½ cup water
2 lbs. fish, boneless, skinless, cut into ½-inch strips
¼ cup vegetable oil

Empty both cans of beans into saucepan. Slowly mix packet of buttermilk dressing and water with beans. Cook until hot (cooking time varies). Fry fish strips in oil until golden brown. Remove from oil; drain on paper towels. Serve on top of cooked beans.

Rob Wodzinski
Iron River, Michigan

The Best Shore Lunch

Fish
Egg, beaten
Flour
Instant potatoes
Cooking oil
Raw potatoes
Lemon pepper
Onions, sliced in rings

To batter fish, dip fillets in egg; coat dipped fillets with flour, then with egg again. Cover fillets with instant mashed potatoes.

Heat oil as hot as possible. Cut up potatoes any way you like them and drop them in oil. Cook halfway and sprinkle lemon pepper while in oil. Take potatoes out. Drop onions into oil. Drop battered fish into oil with onions and cook until flaky.

Mike Malawski
East St. Paul, Manitoba, Canada

Pickled Fish

1½ lbs. fish, cut into bite-size pieces
Vinegar
½ cup white or packed brown sugar
1 cup distilled water
1 cup white vinegar
1 T. pickling spices
4 whole cloves

Soak fish in vinegar. Combine brown sugar, distilled water, white vinegar, pickling spices and cloves in saucepan; heat to boiling. Reduce heat. Cover and simmer for 15 minutes. Let cool to room temperature.

Remove fish from vinegar and rinse in cold water. Place fish chunks in pickling jars and pour cooled pickling solution into jars, completely covering the fish. Seal jars and refrigerate for at least five days to allow the flavors to marinate. Stir fish once during the five-day period to be certain the solution reaches all fish pieces.

The pickled fish should be eaten within six weeks. It must be kept in the pickling solution and refrigerated during this period. Drain fish chunks on paper towels to remove the liquid. Pickled fish is often used as an appetizer or snack. Great with crackers.

Norma Blank
Shawano, Wisconsin

Canned Fish

Per Pint Jar
1 T. vinegar
1 T. ketchup
1 tsp. butter
1 tsp. salt
Fish fillet, cut into bite-size pieces

Put all ingredients into washed pint jars. Pack pieces of fish loosely, leaving 1-inch space at top of jar. Pack without liquid. Place lids on jars; cook in a pressure cooker for 1 ½ hours at 10 pounds, or cook in boiling water bath for 4 hours. Suckers work great but any fish will work.

Randall Webb
Fife Lake, Michigan

Pickled Fish Salad

⅓ cup mayonnaise
1 T. prepared mustard
1 tsp. steak sauce
10 drops hot sauce
1 large tomato
2 small green peppers
2½ cups sliced cucumbers
8 green onions
3 cups well-drained pickled fish
   chunks
4 lettuce leaves

Combine mayonnaise, mustard, steak sauce and hot sauce in bowl. Cut tomato into small chunks; remove seeds and juice. Place in separate large bowl. Cut green pepper into thin rings, removing the inside veins. Add green pepper to the bowl along with cucumbers and green onions. Remove fish from pickling solution; drain well on paper towels, removing all particles of spice. Add fish chunks to the bowl with all the vegetables. Add mayonnaise mixture and toss until well combined. Place lettuce leaves on four plates and divide the salad between the plates. Serve with hot buttered rolls.

Norma Blank
Shawano, Wisconsin

Fish Livers

Fish (northern pike is best, but any
   fish will do)
Pancake flour
Canola oil

Carefully cut the gall bladder from the liver when cleaning fish. Dredge the liver in pancake flour. Deep fry in canola oil (no cholesterol) for 2 to 3 minutes, or until nice and brown. Do not overcook. The livers must be used fresh—once frozen they taste very fishy.

George Dougherty Jr.
Belle Plaine, Iowa

Tim's Pickled Fish

Fish fillets, cut into bite-size pieces
Brine (see recipe below)
1 cup white vinegar
2 raw onions, sliced
Pickling solution (see recipe below)
¼ cup pickling spice

Brine
½ cup salt (not iodized) to 1 qt.
   water

Pickling Solution
(This amount should be enough for
   approximately 4 to 5 lbs. of fillets)
3 cups sugar
4 cups white vinegar

Place chunked fillets of fish into crock with brine for 24 hours. Make sure to cover all fillets completely with brine solution; refrigerate. Drain brine after 24 hours. Cover fillets completely with white vinegar and refrigerate for 12 hours. Drain vinegar; don't reuse for your pickling solution. Pack the fish chunks in jars and add raw onion slices in alternate layers with fish. Prepare the pickling solution; dissolve sugar in white vinegar. Heat, then cool (do not boil here). Add wine, onions and pickling spice. Bring to a boil, then cool. Add enough pickling solution to cover the fish. Place lids on jars and refrigerate. Give fillets a few hours to sit in the jars before eating.

Note: Use with crappies, sunfish (bluegills), northern pike.

Tim Rongstad
Woodbury, Minnesota

Sweet Pepper Pickled Fish

2 to 3 lbs. any freshwater fish fillets, skin removed
8 cups apple cider vinegar
1½ cups vinegar
¼ cup canning or pickling salt
1 cup sugar
3 T. mixed pickled spices
½ cup chopped red pepper
1 large white onion, sliced

Freeze fish for 48 hours at 0°F. Cut into 2-inch pieces; set aside. In large glass mixing bowl, combine vinegars and salt. Stir until salt is almost dissolved. Add fish; cover with plastic wrap. Refrigerate 2 days. With slotted spoon, remove fish from brine. Reserve 3 cups brine. Rinse fish with cold water until rinse water is clear. Cover and chill fish. Pour reserved brine into 4-quart saucepan. Add sugar, spices and red peppers. Bring mixture to a boil over medium-high heat, stirring constantly until sugar is dissolved. Remove from heat. Cool completely. In two 1-quart jars, alternately layer fish and onion. Pour pickling mixture over fish to cover. Seal jars using two-part sealing lids. Refrigerate 1 week before serving. Store in refrigerator no longer than 4 weeks.

Joel Bender
Brill, Wisconsin

Simple Pickled Fish

2 qts. fish fillets, cut into bite-size pieces
White vinegar
Onion, sliced

Brine
1¼ cups sugar
2½ cups white vinegar
2 T. pickling spice

Put fish in stone crock and cover with white vinegar. Let stand 6 to 7 days in refrigerator; stir daily. Drain; rinse well. Let stand in ice water for 30 minutes to 1 hour. Drain. Put fish in jars; alternate layering with onions. Pour brine over fish, cover jars and refrigerate. Ready to eat after 24 to 48 hours. Tastes even better after a few weeks.

Garland Zimmerman
Malden, Missouri

Open-Flame Fish Boil Fun-Do

Fish fillets, skin on or off
Seasoning, to taste
2 T. lemon juice
¼ cup water
1 T. butter

Take 2 square sheets of aluminum foil and place shiny side up on top of each other. Season fillets well and place one or two in middle of foil. Fold up all four sides of the foil, pinch and roll to make a "pan" around fillets. Pour lemon juice over fish. Add water and butter to foil pan. Pinch and roll all sides together to make a closed tent. Leave 3-inch space above fish to take up and hold steam. Cook on hot open flame or grill for 10 to 15 minutes. Remove and open top of tent to let out steam. Test with fork; it should flake easily. You can do the same to your vegetables, too.

Ray Kalisz
Battle Creek, Michigan

Sweet Pepper Pickled Fish

Jim's Fish Grill

2 lemons, sliced
1 medium tomato, sliced
6 slices zucchini
6 slices yellow squash
1 medium green pepper, sliced
   lengthways (julienne)
4 oz. butter, sliced
6 to 8 fillets, your choice of bluegill,
   bass, trout, catfish, etc.
1 tsp. Old Bay seasoning
½ tsp. seasoned salt
½ tsp. black pepper
1 oz. white wine

Line 1 sliced lemon in bottom of pie pan. Place half of all sliced vegetables on top of lemon. Place 2 ounces of butter on vegetables. Lay fish fillets on top of bed of vegetables. Take remaining vegetables and put on top of fish. Sprinkle Old Bay, seasoned salt and pepper on fish/vegetables. Add white wine and remaining 2 ounces butter. Place last sliced lemon layer on top of everything. Cover entire pie pan with large piece of foil to make a pouch. Cook on high on grill 20 minutes or until done.

James Mullen
E. Meredith, New York

Grilled Garlic & Butter Fish

Fish fillets
Butter
Salt, to taste
Pepper, to taste
Fresh garlic, chopped
Onion, chopped

Place fish on aluminum foil. Spread butter over fish; sprinkle with salt and pepper and any other seasonings you prefer. Put butter, garlic and onion on top of fish. Wrap it up with foil, place on grill and cook until fish is tender and flaky. Remove and serve.

Kirk Baird
Douglass, Kansas

Fish in Foil

Fish fillets
Butter or margarine
Lemon juice
Salt, to taste
Pepper, to taste
Paprika
Onion powder

Place fillets on large piece of aluminum foil. Melt butter and pour over fish. Squeeze some lemon juice on fillets. Lightly salt and pepper. Sprinkle with small amount of paprika and onion powder. Fold foil over fillets and fold edges together. Place the package on grill. Turn often to keep from burning. Fish should be cooked in about 10 minutes.

Allan H. Sly
Spooner, Wisconsin

Jim's Fish Grill

Ken's Fried Fish

Vegetable oil
1 cup cornmeal
2 T. Bisquick
1 tsp. salt
Fish fillets

Place ½-inch layer of vegetable oil in large iron skillet. Heat oil until it spatters when you drop a bead of water in it. Place cornmeal, Bisquick and salt in 1-gallon plastic bag and shake well. Place enough fillets in the bag to fill skillet, and shake well to ensure a good coating. Using tongs, drop fish into hot oil and cook until golden brown on one side; then turn them over with spatula. Turn heat down as you flip fillets, but turn it back up before you start next batch. Brown other side; remove and drain well on several paper towels. Store the plastic bag of cornmeal mixture in refrigerator for the next meal.

Fish preparation note: People tell me that my fried fish tastes better than any other. This is not by accident. When filleting fish, place fillets in a pan of extremely cold water. When finished filleting, squeeze fillets until pan of water is discolored with oil and blood. Put fillets in fresh water and repeat process until there is no more blood or oil in them. For stripers (white bass) and sheepshead, fillet off skin and bones, then make a V-cut along the outside of each side and remove dark red streak. Repeat squeezing process and then soak the fillets in milk overnight in the refrigerator.

Kenneth Finch
Minot, Maine

Southern Pan-Fried Fish

2 to 3 lbs. fish
1 cup shortening
2 T. salt
½ cup cornmeal

Cut fish into serving-size pieces. Heat shortening in skillet over medium heat. Combine salt and cornmeal. Roll fish in mixture. Fry in hot shortening for 3 minutes or until delicately browned. Makes 4 servings.

Ryan Wilson
Cypress, Texas

Crispy Fish Fillets

2 lbs. fish fillets
¾ cup beer
1 T. oil
1 tsp. hot sauce
1 egg
1 cup packaged baking mix
Salt, optional

Cut fish into serving-size pieces. Pat dry with paper towels; set aside. Combine beer, oil, hot sauce, egg and baking mix. Blend well. Pour oil 1 inch deep in heavy skillet. Heat to 375°F. Dip fish into batter and fry in hot oil until golden brown on each side, about 5 minutes. Drain on paper towels and sprinkle with salt, if desired. Serve immediately. Makes 6 to 8 servings.

Note: Club soda may be used instead of beer.

Mary Houchin
Swansea, Illinois

Pan-Fried Fish

Flour
Italian bread crumbs
Fish, deboned or whole
Salt, to taste

Combine one part flour and two parts bread crumbs. Wet down fish, salt both sides and coat with flour mixture. Fry on low to medium heat until golden brown.

Jo Carey & Marvin Carey Sr.
Sacramento, California

Beer-Battered Fish

Fish
Beer
Lemon juice
Bread crumbs
Salt, to taste
Pepper, to taste
Mrs. Dash Garlic & Herb
Vegetable oil

Prepare and clean your choice of fish. Soak it in mixture of beer and lemon juice. Remove fish from mixture and heavily coat with bread crumbs, salt, pepper and Mrs. Dash. You may use other seasonings if you prefer. Heat vegetable oil in skillet. When oil gets hot, add fish to skillet and fry until golden brown. Remove and serve.

Kirk Baird
Douglass, Kansas

Fried Fish

1 lb. fresh fish fillets
2 eggs
¼ cup beer
1 cup cornmeal
1 cup flour
1 T. seasoning or spices

Cut fillets into serving-size pieces. Mix eggs and beer until frothy; pour on fish fillets. Mix all dry ingredients together; place in plastic bag. Add fish to dry mixture one piece at a time. Remove fish and place on wax paper or paper plate with some of the dry mix on bottom. Repeat until all fish is coated. Recoat if necessary before cooking in hot oil. Small portions only take a few minutes to brown. Turn if necessary. Place fish on wire rack in warm oven or place on paper bag to drain.

Kim Pendleton
Naples, Florida

Cranberry Glazed Fish Steaks

Cranberry Glazed Fish Steaks

1 (16-oz.) can whole berry cranberry sauce
¼ cup freshly squeezed lemon juice (or lemon juice from concentrate)
3 T. brown sugar
1 tsp. cornstarch
3½ lbs. fish steaks, ¾ to 1 inch thick (salmon, halibut, snapper)

Mustard Butter
½ cup butter or margarine, melted
1½ tsp. salt
1 tsp. prepared mustard
2 tsp. lemon juice
Dash of pepper

In small saucepan, combine cranberry sauce, lemon juice, brown sugar and cornstarch. Cook and stir over medium heat until thickened, about 5 minutes. Set oven to broil. Place fish on lightly greased broiler pan. Broil 2 to 3 inches from heat for 5 to 8 minutes on each side (basting frequently with mustard butter) or until fish flakes easily with fork. Remove fish from oven, spoon half the sauce over fish. Reduce heat to 325°F; bake for 5 minutes more. Spoon remaining sauce over fish; return to oven for 3 to 8 minutes. Makes 7 to 8 servings.

Mustard Butter:
Combine all ingredients together in bowl; mix well.

Joseph Amey
N. Highlands, California

Fish Grill

Fish fillets (walleye, catfish, perch, crappie, panfish, etc.)
Salt, to taste
Pepper, to taste
Onion, chopped
Green pepper, chopped
Butter
Lemon juice

Place ½ pound of fish fillets (or pieces of fish) on square piece of aluminum foil. Sprinkle with salt and pepper and whatever other seasonings you prefer. Add onion and green pepper. Put butter and lemon juice on top. Roll up foil, pinching sides together to seal in butter and lemon juice while cooking. Grill each side for about 4 to 5 minutes, depending on thickness.

Michael Flynn
Hendersonville, Tennessee

Garden Baked Whitefish

2 lbs. whitefish fillets
⅛ tsp. pepper
1 egg white
½ tsp. salt (optional)
¼ cup mayonnaise
¼ tsp. dill weed
½ tsp. onion juice or 1 tsp. grated onion

Preheat oven to 425°F. Spray 13 x 9 x 2-inch baking dish with nonstick cooking spray. Place fish in baking pan; sprinkle with pepper. Beat egg white with salt, if desired, until stiff peaks form. Fold in the mayonnaise, dill weed and onion juice; spoon over fish. Bake, uncovered for 15 to 20 minutes or until topping is puffed and fish flakes easily.

Diabetes Exchange:
Prepare with light mayonnaise and without salt. One serving equals 3 lean meat, ½ fat, also 201 calories, 165 mg sodium, 70 mg cholesterol, 1 gram carbohydrate, 23 grams protein and 11 grams fat.

Norma Blank
Shawano, Wisconsin

Grilled Fish Steaks with Avocado Sauce

Mustard Butter
½ cup butter or margarine, melted
1½ tsp. salt
1 tsp. prepared mustard
2 tsp. lemon juice
Dash of pepper

3 lbs. fish steaks, 1 inch thick
    (salmon, tuna, halibut, etc.)

Avocado Sauce
1 small, ripe avocado, peeled and
    pitted
⅓ cup dairy sour cream
1 tsp. lemon juice
¼ tsp. salt
Few drops of red pepper sauce

Prepare Mustard butter (see recipe below). Place fish on lightly greased grill (or use hinged grill for easier turning). Cook fish 4 inches from medium-hot coals. Cook for 6-8 minutes on each side or until fish flakes easily with fork. Baste frequently with mustard butter. Serve with avocado sauce.

Mustard Butter:
Combine all ingredients together in bowl; mix well.

Avocado Sauce:
Mix all ingredients in blender or beat with rotary beater until smooth.

Joseph Amey
N. Highlands, California

Steamed Hawaiian No-Name & Wild Egg Drop Soup

7 cups water
½ cup plus 1 T. finely chopped wild
    onions
4 ears fresh corn
Peck of watercress
Tarragon, to taste
12 fish fillets
Salt, to taste
Pepper, to taste
Nutmeg, to taste
3 egg whites

Place water and ½ cup chopped onion in Dutch oven. Husk corn; cut to make cobs equal to diameter of top of Dutch oven. Oven is tapered so as to force corn to fit laterally an inch above water level. Place 2 ears one direction, and 2 more on top of lower layer perpendicularly. On top of corn, layer watercress; season liberally with tarragon. Lightly season fish fillets with tarragon, salt and pepper; place on top of watercress. Alternate this process of layers of watercress and fillets so as to end with layer of watercress. Boil and steam 10 minutes with lid slightly opened to allow some steam to rise. Remove layers with 2 forks; serve separated on plates. Re-season each ingredient with tarragon, salt and pepper; sprinkle small amount of nutmeg on the greens. Taste remaining liquid; season to taste. Stir liquid; gradually add egg whites. Eggs will cook rapidly. Serve liquid in soup bowls; sprinkle with remaining tablespoon of chopped uncooked onion as garnish.

Charles S. Haines
Mission Viejo, California

*Grilled Fish Steaks
with Avocado Sauce*

Maine-Style Fish Chowder

6 medium potatoes, diced
2 medium onions, diced
3 cloves garlic, diced
2 lbs. fish fillets, whole (bass, white perch, crappie)
1 qt. whole milk
1 can evaporated milk
Salt, to taste
Pepper, to taste
⅛ lb. butter
¼ lb. salt pork, diced

Place potatoes, onions and garlic in Dutch oven with enough water to cover vegetables. Boil until tender. While boiling, put fish in colander; steam over vegetables. Add steamed fish to kettle. Add whole milk, canned milk, salt, pepper and butter. Place salt pork in skillet; fry on low heat until brown. Add pork and drippings to Dutch oven. Heat chowder for 30 minutes, being careful not to boil and curdle the milk.

Bruce Thibeault
Peru, Maine

Easy Shore Lunch Fish Soup

2 cloves garlic, crushed
¼ cup olive oil
2 lbs. striper, catfish or carp
3 cups water
½ tsp. oregano
Salt, to taste
1 T. chopped parsley
Pinch of paprika
1 T. chopped fennel tops

In large skillet, sauté garlic in oil. Add fish, water, oregano, salt, parsley, paprika and fennel tops to skillet; simmer until fish is cooked through.

Rich Beaudry
Pagosa Springs, Colorado

White Fish in Sweet & Sour Sauce

1 cup unflavored bread crumbs
2 eggs
Salt, to taste
4 (6 oz.) white fish fillets
3 T. butter
2 T. olive oil
1 cup dry white wine
2 T. sugar
3 T. lemon juice

Spread bread crumbs on piece of aluminum foil. Lightly beat eggs; add salt if desired. Dip fish in egg; coat with bread crumbs. Press crumbs onto fish completely. Let stand 10 minutes. Melt 2 tablespoons butter with oil in large skillet. When butter foams, add fish. Cook over medium heat 2 minutes on each side or until fish is lightly golden. Place fish on serving dishes; keep warm in low-heated oven while finishing the sauce. Add wine to skillet; stir over high heat. When wine is almost all reduced, add remaining tablespoon of butter, sugar and lemon juice. Season with salt. Cook and stir until the sauce has medium-thick, glazy consistency. Spoon over fish; serve.

Gordon Kremer
Sacramento, California

Deep-Fried Fish Balls

1 lb. fish fillets
2 large potatoes
4 cups salted water
1 egg, beaten
1 tsp. minced onion
½ tsp. salt
¼ tsp. pepper
½ tsp. dry mustard
1 tsp. lemon juice
2 T. parsley
Oil

Place fish and potatoes in saucepan with salted water; bring to a boil. Simmer for 20 minutes until fish and potatoes are tender. Drain. Place fish and potatoes in large bowl; mash and stir gently to mix them. Add egg, onion, salt, pepper, mustard, lemon juice and parsley. Mix well. Form fish mixture into 2-inch balls. Heat oil to 375°F in deep skillet or deep fryer. Cook fish balls a few at a time, until golden brown. Drain and place on heated platter until all fish balls have been cooked. Serve.

Michael Bragg
Point Pleasant, West Virginia

Quick Fried Fish Recipe

3½ lbs. fish, dressed, washed and
    dried
Salt, to taste
1 egg, beaten
Flour
¼ lb. butter

Salt fish inside and out. Dip fish into beaten egg and then dip into flour. Heat butter in skillet. Fry fish in butter until fish is light brown in color. Add melted butter as a gravy to fish.

Sean Cunningham
Taylor, Texas

Bonnie Mae's Fish Fillets

1 cup beer
1 cup flour
4 tsp. cornstarch
1 egg
1 tsp. salt
1 tsp. baking soda
¼ tsp. garlic powder
8 fish fillets
¼ cup salad oil

Mix all ingredients except fish and oil together to make batter. Dip fish in batter and fry in oil at 350°F until golden brown.

Note: You may replace 1 cup beer with 1 cup water instead.

Bob Rhoads
Mount Vernon, Indiana

Walleye & Pike

Everyone has a favorite fish to eat. Even if it's not your personal favorite, few people would argue against a walleye—so snowy-white-fleshed and mild-flavored—as one of the finest-eating fish that swims. Same with pike, although they're often a bit more of a stretch when it comes to convincing an angler that the toothy, muscle-bound, slimy-green predator thrashing about on your line has some of the whitest and tastiest fish flesh around; you just have to work around the pesky Y-bones. Yes, walleye and pike are fun to fish for, and fun to eat when the resource can spare a fish or two.

Croix Pike,
Page 59

Walleye Jerome

Walleye Jerome

2 tomatoes, peeled and thinly sliced
Bread crumbs, 2 T. per serving
Salt, to taste
Pepper, to taste
2 lbs. walleye fillets
½ cup white port wine
½ stick butter
3 shallots, chopped
1 T. lemon juice
Parmesan cheese, grated
Paprika
Almonds, slivered (optional)

In large baking pan, layer tomatoes, bread crumbs, salt and pepper; top with fillets. In saucepan, heat port wine, butter and shallots; boil for 2 minutes. Add lemon juice. Pour over fillets and sprinkle with Parmesan cheese, paprika and almonds, if desired. Bake at 350°F for 20 to 30 minutes.

David J. Carolan
Elkader, Iowa

Bacon & Onion Walleye

1 T. butter
1 lb. walleye fillets
2 T. French onion dip
1 small onion, chopped
2 T. bacon bits
Dash of seasoned salt
Dash of garlic salt

Heat grill to medium heat. Lay out 2 sheets of aluminum foil. Spread butter on foil. Lay out fillets in single layer on foil; spread French onion dip on top of fillets. Sprinkle onion and bacon bits on top of fillets; season with seasoned salt and garlic salt. Lay third piece of aluminum foil on top; roll in sides and ends. Grill fish for 10 to 15 minutes.

Tom Valko
Marysville, Michigan

Honey-Fried Walleye

1 egg
1 tsp. plus additional honey
1 cup coarsely crushed saltines (22 to 25 crackers)
⅓ cup flour
¼ tsp. salt
¼ tsp. pepper
4 to 6 walleye fillets, skin removed
Vegetable oil

In small bowl, beat egg and 1 teaspoon honey. In separate bowl, combine cracker crumbs, flour, salt and pepper. Dip fillets in egg mixture; coat with cracker mixture. In large skillet, heat ¼ inch oil. Fry fish over medium-high heat 3 to 4 minutes on each side or until fish flakes easily. Drizzle with additional honey.

Norma A. Blank
Shawano, Wisconsin

Campfire Delight Walleye

1 lb. walleye fillets
2 T. butter, softened
1 T. lemon juice
1 T. fresh basil or ½ tsp. dried basil
1 tsp. lemon pepper seasoning
½ tsp. garlic salt
4 oz. fresh mushrooms, sliced

Spray 18 x 18-inch piece of aluminum foil with nonstick cooking spray. Place fillets in foil. Spread butter on top. Sprinkle with lemon juice, basil, lemon pepper and garlic salt. Top with mushrooms. Bring opposite edges of foil together, fold down several times. Fold remaining edges toward fish; seal tightly. Grill, covered, over hot coals for 10 to 14 minutes, turning once, until fish flakes easily.

Gordon Kremer
Sacramento, California

Matt's Famous Beer-Battered Walleye

¾ cup milk
1 cup plus additional flour
1 tsp. salt
1 tsp. black pepper
½ tsp. cayenne pepper
½ tsp. paprika
¼ tsp. baking soda
1 egg
1½ lbs. walleye fillets
⅓ cup light beer
Vegetable oil

Mix milk, 1 cup flour, salt, peppers, paprika, baking soda and egg until smooth. Set aside for 10 to 15 minutes. Cut walleye fillets into 1-inch strips (3 inches long). Rinse under cold water, then pat dry. Place strips in small bowl; fill with beer until covered. Chill 25 to 30 minutes. Remove walleye strips from beer, lightly roll in flour, then quickly submerge in batter. Shake off excess and drop into hot oil. Fry until golden brown.

Matthew Radzialowski
Wixom, Michigan

Blackened Walleye

1 tsp. salt
1 tsp. black pepper
1 tsp. garlic powder
1 tsp. paprika
1 tsp. onion powder
½ tsp. white pepper
½ tsp. oregano
½ tsp. thyme
½ tsp. cayenne pepper
2 lbs. walleye fillets
1 cup butter, melted

Place large cast-iron skillet on camp stove, gas barbecue side burner or directly on bed of hot coals. The skillet should remain on heat until extremely hot. In the meantime, blend salt, pepper, garlic powder, paprika, onion powder, white pepper, oregano, thyme and cayenne pepper. When skillet is ready, coat fillets with melted butter. Roll fillets in seasoning until they are well coated. Lay fillets in skillet; cook 2 minutes. Remove and serve.

Allan H. Sly
Spooner, Wisconsin

Pickled Walleye

16 oz. walleye
2 T. Ball 100% natural canning and
    pickling salt
2½ cups water
1 cup white wine vinegar
½ cup freshly squeezed lemon juice
½ tsp. Angostura Romatic bitters
¼ tsp. Old Bay seasoning

Fillet walleye; cut into 1-inch cubes. Place in quart jar. Add pickling salt to water; pour over fish cubes. Refrigerate 2 days. Drain and wash. Place cubed walleye in quart jar. Mix vinegar, lemon juice, bitters and Old Bay seasoning together. Pour over walleye cubes; cap and refrigerate 3 days.

Garland Zimmerman
Malden, Missouri

Batter-Fried Walleye or Northern Pike

Oil
Salt, to taste
Pepper, to taste
2 lbs. walleye fillets
3 cups flour
1 onion, chopped
2 T. parsley flakes
2 T. lemon juice
Garlic salt, to taste
Onion salt, to taste
2 cans beer
4 cups corn flakes

In deep cast-iron skillet, heat oil to high temperature. Use enough oil so fillets can float. Salt and pepper fillets. Mix flour, onion, parsley, lemon juice, garlic salt and onion salt. Gradually stir in one can of beer. Crush corn flakes; add to mixture while stirring. Beat to consistency of light pancake batter using as much of the second can of beer as necessary. Batter fillets; drop very gently into hot oil. Turn fillets over when they are golden brown.

John P. Pelrine
Chicago, Illinois

Baked Stuffed Walleye

3 lbs. walleye, whole
Salt, to taste
Pepper, to taste
1 box stuffing mix
1 small can oysters, with juice
¾ cup milk
⅛ tsp. ground sage
Small white onion, sliced
4 strips bacon
Lemon juice, to taste

Preheat oven to 250°F. Thoroughly clean walleye. Cut off head, tail and dorsal fin. Salt and pepper inside and out. Combine stuffing, oysters, milk and sage to make moist stuffing mix. Stuff cavity of walleye; sew flaps together. Place fish in shallow pan; lay onion slices on top. Place bacon over onions and drizzle with lemon juice. Bake for 2½ hours, or until meat is white and flakes easily with fork.

Greg Haut
Waukesha, Wisconsin

Walleye Sauté

1 lb. walleye fillets
2 T. vegetable oil
1 cup sliced onions
1 cup julienned carrots
1 cup julienned green pepper
2 tomatoes, peeled and cut into
    wedges
½ tsp. sweet basil
Salt, to taste
Pepper, to taste

Cut fillets into bite-size pieces. Heat oil in large skillet over medium heat. Add onions, carrots and green pepper. Sauté 10 minutes. Add walleye, tomatoes, basil, salt and pepper. Cover and reduce heat; simmer 10 minutes or until fish flakes easily.

Gordon Kremer
Sacramento, California

Sautéed Walleye with Sour Cream & Dill

1 T. unsalted butter
1 T. olive oil
2 walleye fillets
¼ cup flour
¼ cup cornmeal
Salt, to taste
Pepper, to taste
½ cup white wine
6 T. sour cream
2 T. fresh dill, chopped (2 tsp. dry)
1 T. fresh parsley or chives,
    chopped
Dash of lemon, chopped

In large skillet, melt butter and olive oil until foam subsides. Rinse fillets; pat dry. Combine flour, cornmeal, salt and pepper. Dredge fillets in mixture; shake lightly to remove excess. Sauté fillets over medium heat until golden brown. Turn fish; cook until fish flakes easily. Clean skillet; return to medium-high heat. Add wine; cook 5 to 8 minutes, or until reduced by half. Whisk in sour cream until smooth; remove from heat and add dill, parsley and lemon, to taste. Add salt and pepper if desired. Pour sauce over fish; serve immediately.

Norma A. Blank
Shawano, Wisconsin

Salsa Walleye

Walleye
Butter
Seasoned salt
Picante sauce

Poach walleye in water or butter seasoned with seasoned salt. Drain; add mild or medium picante sauce. Chunk fish; mix well.

David Stahlhut
Newnan, Georgia

Walleye Sauté

Walleye Cioppino (Fish Stew)

⅓ cup extra-virgin olive oil
2 cloves garlic, crushed
3 medium onions, diced
4½ cups water
3½ cups canned plum tomatoes
3 T. lemon juice
2 T. sugar
2 tsp. salt
1 tsp. grated lemon rind
½ tsp. pepper
½ tsp. paprika
¼ tsp. dried thyme
¼ tsp. dried basil
1 lb. walleye fillets, cubed

Heat oil in large skillet over medium-high heat. Sauté garlic and onions for 10 minutes. Add water, tomatoes, lemon juice, sugar, salt, lemon rind, pepper, paprika, thyme and basil, stirring occasionally until slightly thickened. Add walleye; simmer 10 to 15 minutes.

Norma A. Blank
Shawano, Wisconsin

Poached Walleye

Walleye fillets
Seasoned salt
1 stick butter
Juice from 1 lemon
Garlic salt, to taste

Poach backs of walleye fillets in water with seasoned salt. Drain well. In separate pan, melt butter, lemon juice and garlic salt. Pour butter mixture lightly over fish chunks.

David Stahlhut
Newnan, Georgia

Garlic Cheeks

3 T. extra-virgin olive oil
3 T. butter
¼ cup finely diced onions
2 T. finely diced garlic (and juice)
10 to 20 walleye cheeks
Dash of salt
Dash of freshly ground black pepper
Splash of white wine

Heat oil and butter until hot (not smoking). Add onions and garlic. Mix and sauté 1 to 2 minutes. Add cheeks; sauté 1 to 2 minutes, stirring often. Add salt, pepper and wine. Sauté until wine evaporates (maximum 2 minutes). Serve on platter with seafood sauce or fresh lemon.

Note: Salmon cheeks may be used in place of walleye cheeks.

David Baxter
Ayton, Ontario, Canada

Pike Stew

3 lbs. pike or muskie fillets
6 lbs. potatoes, cut into ¼-inch-thick
    slices
Butter
8 to 10 bacon slices
Cayenne pepper
Salt, to taste
Pepper, to taste

In large baking dish, alternately layer fish and potatoes, making sure to end with potatoes on top. Dot each layer of fish with butter. Place bacon slices on top. Sprinkle with cayenne pepper, salt and pepper. Cover with water and slow cook until tender. Allow top to brown.

Ray Murley
Oshawa, Ontario, Canada

"Instead of Frying" Fish

1 lb. walleye fillets
¼ cup milk
1 cup crushed potato chips
¼ cup grated Parmesan cheese
¼ tsp. dried thyme
1 T. dry bread crumbs
2 T. butter, melted

Preheat oven to 500°F. Cut fish into serving-size pieces. Place milk in shallow bowl. In separate shallow bowl, combine potato chips, Parmesan cheese and thyme. Dip fish into milk, then coat with potato chip mixture. Spray an 8-inch-square baking dish with nonstick cooking spray; sprinkle with bread crumbs. Place fish on top of bread crumbs; drizzle with butter. Bake, uncovered, for 12 to 14 minutes or until fish flakes easily.

Gordon Kremer
Sacramento, California

Sweet & Sour Fish

3½ to 4 lbs. pike
Salt, to taste
4 gingersnaps, crushed
½ cup brown sugar
¼ cup apple vinegar
¼ cup seedless grapes
1 small onion, chopped
1 lemon, sliced

Clean, slice and salt fish. Let stand in cooler for 2 hours. Boil 20 minutes, drain and bone. Reserve 1 cup of fish stock. Combine fish stock with gingersnaps, brown sugar, apple vinegar, seedless grapes, onion and lemon. Cook until smooth and thick. Pour over fish. Serve cold.

Bob Rhoads
Mount Vernon, Indiana

Walleye Chili

8 lbs. walleye, filleted and cubed
½ clove garlic
3 cans chili beans
3 cans diced tomatoes with green
    chiles
2 medium onions, diced
1 to 2 bottles barbecue sauce

In large skillet sprayed with nonstick cooking spray, sauté fish and garlic. In 6-quart Dutch oven, add chili beans, tomatoes with green chilies, onions and barbecue sauce. Add fish; cook over low heat 2 hours.

Alan Ingold
Miami, Indiana

Croix Pike

Croix Pike

4 pike fillets
Pepper medley or cracked
   peppercorns
1 stick butter
6 cloves garlic, minced
1 lemon, quartered

Heat grill to medium-high heat, or light your charcoal and let it burn down to hot, glowing coals. Grease grill grid with nonstick cooking spray or small amount of olive oil. Coat each side of fish liberally with pepper medley or cracked peppercorns. Sprinkle pepper and work it in, or roll the fish in the pepper.

Melt butter on low-medium heat in small skillet. Add minced garlic; sauté for minute or so. Don't let butter smoke, or brown garlic too much! Squeeze in juice from lemon quarters. Warm up this baste.

Place pike on grill; cook for 5 minutes, brushing regularly with baste. Don't remove the pepper! Flip fish; grill for 2 minutes more, using remaining baste. Adjust cooking times according to fillet thickness; don't overcook!

Tom Carpenter
Plymouth, Minnesota

Baked Walleye

¾ cup chopped onion
¾ cup chopped green pepper
¾ cup chopped celery
1 T. dried parsley flakes
½ tsp. garlic powder
½ tsp. pepper
½ tsp. seasoned salt
1 cup V-8 juice
1 lb. walleye fillets

Preheat oven to 350°F. In saucepan, combine onion, green pepper, celery, parsley, garlic powder, pepper, seasoned salt and V-8 juice. Bring to a boil. Reduce heat and simmer, uncovered, 5 minutes, stirring occasionally, until vegetables are crisp-tender. Place fish in greased 13 x 9 x 2-inch baking pan. Pour vegetable mixture over fish. Cover; bake for 30 minutes or until fish flakes easily.

Norma A. Blank
Shawano, Wisconsin

Quick & Easy Microwave Pike

4 pike fillets
Butter
1 cup diced green pepper
1 cup diced onion

Clean and prepare pike. Lay pike in microwave-safe dish. Butter fish; pour diced peppers and onions over fish. Cook in microwave 8 to 12 minutes.

Joseph Booth
Richland, Michigan

Sugar-Smoked Walleye

Sugar-Smoked Walleye

16½ cups apple juice
¾ cup canning or pickling salt
½ cup plus 1 T. packed brown sugar
6 (8 oz.) walleye fillets, skin on
4 to 6 cups cherry wood chips
1 tsp. maple syrup

In 5-quart glass or plastic container, combine 8 cups apple juice, ¾ cup pickling salt and ¼ cup brown sugar. Stir until salt and sugar are dissolved. Add fillets to brine. Cover and refrigerate 12 hours overnight.

Place wood chips in large mixing bowl. Cover with water. Soak chips 1 hour. Drain and discard brine from fillets; rinse with water. Pat dry and arrange fillets on cooling racks. Air dry 1 hour or until fillets are shiny and dry.

Place oven thermometer in smoker. Add 8 cups apple juice and ¼ cup brown sugar to water pan in smoker. Heat wet smoker with filled water pan 20 minutes or until temperature registers 100°F. Spray smoker racks with nonstick cooking spray. Arrange fillets on prepared racks, spacing at least ½ inch apart. Drain and discard water from wood chips. Smoke fillets with wet chips according to smoker manufacturer's directions (2 to 3 hours) or until fish flakes easily with fork and internal temperature registers 180°F.

In 1-quart saucepan, combine ½ cup apple juice, 1 tablespoon brown sugar and 1 teaspoon maple syrup. Cook over medium heat 2 to 3 minutes or until mixture is hot and sugar is dissolved, stirring frequently. Brush glaze over fillets. Continue smoking 30 minutes to 1 hour, or until glaze is set. Store smoked fish, loosely wrapped, in refrigerator no longer than 2 weeks.

Joel Bednar
Brill, Wisconsin

Pickled Northern Pike

8 cups vinegar
⅝ cup salt
3 to 4 cups bite-size northern pike
  pieces
3 cups sugar
½ box pickling salt
1 large onion, sliced

Mix 4 cups vinegar and salt together. Pour over fish chunks and let stand in refrigerator for 1 week. Rinse; soak 1 hour in cold water. In saucepan, mix remaining 4 cups vinegar with sugar and pickling salt. Bring to a boil; let cool. Put layers of fish and onion in gallon jar. Pour cooled brine over fish and let stand in refrigerator for 3 weeks.

John Pelrine
Chicago, Illinois

Panfish & Bass

Panfish of all kinds are tops on the popularity scale … both for fishing and eating! Bluegills, shellcrackers, perch, crappies—they are white and firm in the pan, sweet and full of taste on the plate. What's more, a guy never has to feel too guilty about keeping a small mess to clean and later eat. Bass, of course, are an "iffier" proposition. But if the waterway's population is healthy and there's a plethora of young fish marauding about, it might not hurt to crop a few off, if regulations permit. Some people wouldn't think of eating a bass … but it is good, not unlike its panfish cousins, in texture and flavor.

Ginger Striped Bass,
Page 76

Poached Crappie Roll with Shrimp Mousseline

Poached Crappie Roll with Shrimp Mousseline

3 crappies (½ to 1 lb. each)
1 lb. shrimp

Poaching Stock
Shrimp shells
½ cup finely diced onion
¼ cup finely diced carrot
¼ cup finely diced celery
3 sprigs fresh thyme
4 parsley stems
6 peppercorns
1 bay leaf
Water
6 oz. dry white vermouth

Mousseline
1 egg white
¼ tsp. salt
White pepper, to taste
6 oz. heavy cream
1 T. chopped parsley

Sauce
2 oz. butter
¼ cup flour, sifted
1½ cups milk
1 T. Parmesan cheese, grated
¼ cup Swiss cheese, grated
¼ tsp. salt
White pepper, to taste

Fillet crappies, trim and cut each fillet in half lengthwise along median line; wrap and refrigerate.

Peel and devein shrimp. Place shells into saucepan with onion, carrot, celery, thyme, parsley stems, peppercorns and bay leaf. Add enough cold water to cover completely. Simmer 30 minutes.

Mousseline:
Set aside 2 to 3 shrimp per person. Place remaining shrimp in food processor. Pulse to a coarse paste. Add egg white, salt, white pepper and cream. Pulse to smooth. Remove from processor and fold in chopped parsley. Lay fillets between 2 sheets plastic wrap with skin side down. Pound fillets with meat mallet until even thickness. Spread thin layer of shrimp mousseline over each fillet and roll from tail end to head end. Place rolls in baking dish. Preheat oven to 350°F.

Strain stock through cheesecloth over bowl or saucepan. Add vermouth to stock then pour into pan with rolls. Cook in oven until almost cooked through. Add shrimp previously set aside about halfway through cooking time, approximately 5 to 15 minutes.

Sauce:
Melt butter on low heat in saucepan. Blend in flour, stir until there are no lumps. Add milk while stirring and increase heat; do not boil. When sauce thickens, add Parmesan and Swiss cheese, stirring to prevent cheese from settling on bottom of pan. When cheese has melted and blended, add salt and white pepper to taste. If sauce is too thick add some poaching liquid, heated heavy cream or milk to thin. Strain through cheesecloth.

To serve, ladle shallow spoonful of sauce onto plate and place 2 to 3 rolls, standing on end, with shrimp into sauce.

Henry L. Tardiff
Bennington, New Hampshire

Crappie Fry

2 lbs. crappie fillets
32 to 40 oz. canola oil
2 to 3 cups cornmeal mix
Seasoned salt, to taste
Cayenne pepper, to taste
Garlic powder, to taste
8 oz. buttermilk

Prepare crappie fillets and cut into finger-size pieces. Place crappie on paper towels to remove moisture from fish; place in refrigerator until ready to cook. Place canola oil in deep fryer or deep skillet and heat to 375 to 400°F. In 1-gallon freezer bag, combine cornmeal mix, seasoned salt, cayenne pepper and garlic powder. Place buttermilk in medium bowl. Take chilled, dry crappie and place in buttermilk until coated thoroughly. Transfer to freezer bag; close bag and shake vigorously. Cook fish in hot cooking oil 3 to 4 minutes or until golden brown. Drain on paper towels.

Will N. Blankenship
Emory, Texas

Baked Bass

4 (8 oz.) bass fillets
½ lemon
1 cup sour cream
½ cup mayonnaise
2 cups sliced mushrooms, sautéed
2 T. butter, melted
Salt, to taste
Pepper, to taste
Paprika

Preheat oven to 350°F. Place each fillet in piece of aluminum foil and season with a squeeze of lemon. Combine sour cream, mayonnaise, mushrooms, butter, salt and pepper. Spoon sour cream mixture over each fillet. Seal foil and bake for 20 minutes, or until done. Broil uncovered for 1 minute to brown. Sprinkle with paprika.

Powell Bait Company
Hull, Georgia

Fried Bluegill Parmesan

1 lb. bluegill fillets
¼ cup flour
1 egg
1½ T. milk
16 oz. saltine crackers, crushed
½ tsp. parsley flakes
½ tsp. sweet basil
¼ tsp. oregano
⅛ tsp. garlic powder
½ cup grated Parmesan cheese
½ cup butter-flavored Crisco

Pat fish dry with paper towels. Dredge fish in flour and shake off excess. In a small bowl, mix egg and milk. In a separate bowl, mix crackers, parsley, basil, oregano, garlic powder and Parmesan cheese. Dip fish in egg mix, then in cracker mix. In skillet, heat Crisco to 425°F. Place breaded fish in oil, skin side up. Fry until golden brown.

Henry R. Andrews
Osage Beach, Missouri

Bass Pinecone Magic

3 lbs. striped bass fillets with skins
Salt, to taste
Pepper, to taste
Marjoram, to taste
Paprika, to taste
½ lb. butter
Several pinecones

Sprinkle fillets with seasonings. Grill over hot coals, skinside down. Dot with butter. Grill 10 to 12 minutes; turn. Add several pinecones to hot charcoal to flavor fish. Turn fillets skinside down when pinecones begin to brown. Add butter as needed to keep fillets moist. Grill until fish flakes easily.

Ryan Wilson
Cypress, Texas

Midwest Crappie Supreme

2 eggs
½ cup milk
1 cup powdered pancake mix
Salt, to taste
Pepper, to taste
2 lbs. crappie fillets

Beat eggs; mix well with milk. In separate bowl, combine pancake mix, salt and pepper. Dip fillets in egg/milk mixture, then coat with pancake mixture. Drop fillets into deep fryer; cook until golden brown.

William R. Baker
Deltona, Florida

Bubbling Panfish Bake

¼ cup chopped onion
2 T. butter
1 can condensed cream of mush-
    room soup
1 cup milk
1 cup shredded cheddar cheese
4 cups cooked macaroni
¾ lb. panfish fillets
2 T. buttered bread crumbs

Cook onion in butter until tender. Add soup, milk and ¾ cup of cheese. Fold in macaroni and fish. Pour into 1½-quart baking dish; top with bread crumbs and remaining cheese. Bake for 35 minutes or until bubbling and lightly browned.

Ray Murley
Oshawa, Ontario, Canada

Crispy Fried Crappie

½ cup oil
8 crappie fillets
1 cup cornmeal
½ cup flour
Salt, to taste
Pepper, to taste

Heat oil in skillet to medium-high heat. In small bowl, mix together cornmeal, flour, salt and pepper. Score fillets and roll in cornmeal mix, covering completely. Drop fillets in hot skillet and fry each side until light brown.

Leonard Mincks
Halfway, Missouri

Bluegill Sauté

6 oz. butter
12 bluegill fillets
1 cup flour
⅓ cup diced celery
½ bunch green onions, chopped
½ large green pepper, diced
6 oz. mushrooms, quartered
½ tsp. seasoned salt
½ tsp. white pepper
1 tsp. Old Bay seasoning
3 T. ketchup
2 oz. white wine
1 T. chopped fresh parsley

Melt butter in saucepan over medium-high heat. Dredge bluegill fillets in flour and cook in butter until done. Place on tray; keep warm in oven. In same saucepan, add celery, onions and green pepper; cook 3 minutes. Add mushrooms and cook 2 additional minutes. Stir in seasoned salt, pepper, Old Bay seasoning, ketchup and white wine. Cover and simmer over low heat until vegetables are tender. Remove from heat and pour over bluegill fillets. Sprinkle with parsley.

James Mullen
East Meredith, New York

Poor Man's Lobster

1 tsp. salt
2 slices lemon, peel intact
2 qts. water
3 to 4 crappie fillets, cut into bite-size pieces
½ cup garlic butter

Boil salt and lemon slices in water; add fish pieces and boil 2 minutes. Drain and dip in garlic butter.

Josh Krause
Manhattan, Kansas

Mustard-Fried Bluegill

12 bluegill fillets
1 (16-oz.) carton sour cream
1 cup prepared mustard
3 cups yellow cornmeal
Salt, to taste
Pepper, to taste
Peanut oil

Scale and clean bluegills. Coat fish with sour cream and mustard; let stand 20 minutes in refrigerator. Season cornmeal with salt and pepper. Dredge fish in mixture. Deep fry in skillet with hot peanut oil until golden brown.

Henry R. Andrews
Osage Beach, Missouri

Bluegill Sauté

Chef Jeff's Classic Fish Cuisine

2 T. olive oil
2 cups flour
1 tsp. salt
1 tsp. pepper
6 to 8 panfish fillets
1 tsp. fresh garlic or 1½ tsp. garlic
   powder
1 T. minced shallots
1 cup whole butter
½ cup cooked, quartered artichokes
1 lemon, cut into rings

In large saucepan, heat olive oil until smoking. Season flour with salt and pepper; dust fish and place in hot oil. Cook until brown, turning once. Remove and place on serving plate. Add garlic and shallots to saucepan. Remove garlic when browned. Add ½ cup butter, artichokes and lemon rings. Heat 2 to 3 minutes. Remove lemon rings. Remove saucepan from heat. Slowly stir in remaining ½ cup butter until cools to creamy sauce. Pour over fish.

Jeff S. Mueller
North Sioux City, South Dakota

Perch Delight

10 to 12 medium-size perch fillets
2 eggs, well beaten
3 T. flour
5 T. shortening
Salt, to taste
Pepper, to taste
Paprika, to taste
½ cup tomato paste
1 tsp. cornstarch
½ cup milk

Dip fish in egg, then roll in flour. Melt shortening; brown fillets over medium heat. Reduce heat to low. Season fillets with salt, pepper and paprika. Continue cooking 20 more minutes. Remove fillets to serving platter. Mix tomato paste, cornstarch and milk; add to drippings in skillet. Bring to a boil; pour over fillets.

Ray Murley
Oshawa, Ontario, Canada

Spicy Popcorn Panfish

2 eggs
2 tsp. lemon juice
1 tsp. hot sauce
1 tsp. cayenne pepper
½ cup crushed corn flakes
½ cup flour
Dash of cayenne pepper
Dash of lemon pepper
Dash of salt
Panfish fillets, cut into bite-size
   pieces

In small bowl, beat eggs, lemon juice, hot sauce and cayenne pepper well. In separate bowl, mix corn flakes, flour, cayenne pepper, lemon pepper and salt. Dip fish pieces into egg mixture, then into flour mixture. Repeat dipping process and fry in hot oil 7 to 10 minutes or until golden brown. Drain on paper towels.

Jennifer Ann Kunze
Grand Rapids, Minnesota

Chef Jeff's Classic Fish Cuisine

Perch de Jahner

2 T. butter
1 clove garlic, peeled and minced
Dash of salt
1 T. minced chives
1 T. minced Italian parsley
2 T. dry sherry
White pepper, to taste
½ lb. perch fillets
¼ cup bread crumbs

Preheat oven to 375°F. In medium skillet, melt butter; add garlic and sauté 5 minutes over low heat until tender. Stir in salt, chives, parsley and sherry. Season with white pepper. Arrange perch fillets in buttered shallow pan. Pour butter mixture over fish. Sprinkle with bread crumbs. Bake for 10 minutes or until fish and bread crumbs are golden.

Gordon Kremer & Harvey Jahner
Sacramento, California

Fish Cakes

1 T. butter
1 large onion, finely diced
1 egg, hard boiled
20 to 25 saltine crackers, crushed
1 cup milk, scalded
1 T. Worcestershire sauce
½ tsp. mustard
¼ tsp. paprika
½ lb. panfish, cooked, deboned
Seasoned bread crumbs
Vegetable oil

Heat butter in skillet and sauté onion until translucent; set aside. Peel and mash egg with fork; set aside. Add crackers to scalded milk until moistened and lightly thickened. Add onions, egg, Worcestershire sauce, mustard, paprika and fish to cracker mixture. Stir until well mixed. Take approximately 1 to 2 tablespoons of mixture and form into patties about ¼ inch thick. Dip patties into seasoned bread crumbs. Fry each patty in vegetable oil until golden brown on both sides.

Michael A. Miller
Palm, Pennsylvania

Panfish Pizza

Panfish fillets
Italian dressing
Potato chips, crushed
Mozzarella cheese

Marinate fillets in Italian dressing for 1 hour. Preheat oven to 300°F. Cover baking sheet with aluminum foil; lightly coat with nonstick cooking spray. Drain fillets and place close together on baking sheet. Sprinkle fillets liberally with potato chips and cheese. Bake for 10 to 15 minutes or until completely cooked.

Steve Ward
Marion, Ohio

River Panfish Delight

½ cup flour
⅛ tsp. salt
⅛ tsp. pepper
⅛ tsp. thyme
⅛ tsp. marjoram
1 egg, beaten
⅛ cup evaporated milk
½ cup crushed crackers
1 lb. panfish fillets

In small bowl, combine flour, salt, pepper, thyme and marjoram. In separate bowl, combine egg and milk together. Stir crackers into flour mixture. Dip fillets in egg mixture; then roll in flour mix. Drop coated fillets into hot oil and cook until golden brown, turning once.

Ray Murley
Oshawa, Ontario, Canada

Bob's Easy-Bake Low-Fat Crappie

2 lbs. crappie fillets
Juice from 1 lemon
1 lb. cherry tomatoes, cut in half
1 medium onion, thinly sliced
1 cup flour
2 tsp. chopped parsley
Salt, to taste
Pepper, to taste

Preheat oven to 350°F. Spray baking pan with nonstick cooking spray. Spread fillets skin side down in pan. Sprinkle lemon juice over fish. In medium bowl, mix together tomatoes, onion and flour with a little water. Pour over fish, sprinkle with parsley, salt and pepper; cover with foil. Bake for 20 to 45 minutes.

Note: Instead of 1 pound of cherry tomatoes, you may substitute sliced, whole tomatoes or canned tomatoes.

Robert Kukuvka
Rockaway, New Jersey

Panfish Tempura

1 cup self-rising flour
2 eggs, beaten
Cold water
Panfish, cleaned and skinned
Oil

In small bowl, mix together flour, eggs and water. Dip fish in batter and drop in hot oil in skillet. Cook briefly until batter is crispy. Remove fish; drain on paper towels.

Bob Kinzie
Bethesda, Maryland

Fried Crappie Fingers with Sauce

Fried Crappie Fingers with Sauce

Oil
2 cups self-rising cornmeal
2 T. flour
Pepper, to taste
4 eggs, beaten
3 lbs. crappie fillets, cut into bite-
   size pieces

Red Dipping Sauce
1½ cups ketchup
2 T. brown sugar
2 T. Worcestershire sauce
1 tsp. dry mustard
⅓ cup whiskey

In large saucepan, heat oil. In small bowl, combine cornmeal, flour and pepper. Place beaten eggs in separate bowl. Dry fillets on paper towels. Dredge fillets in eggs, then in cornmeal mixture. Repeat dipping process. Let sit for 2 minutes. Fry until golden brown.

Red Dipping Sauce:
In small saucepan, mix together ketchup, brown sugar, Worcestershire sauce and dry mustard. Bring to a boil, stirring occasionally. Stir in whiskey and simmer 5 minutes. Refrigerate until crappie fingers are done cooking.

John P. Pelrine
Chicago, Illinois

Pan-Fried Crappie

10 to 12 crappie fillets
1 egg
½ cup milk
½ cup cornmeal
½ cup Italian bread crumbs
2 T. Romano cheese, grated

In 12-inch skillet, heat ⅜ inch cooking oil on medium-high heat. In small bowl, mix together egg and milk. In separate bowl, combine cornmeal, bread crumbs and cheese. Dip fillets in egg mixture, then roll in bread crumb mixture. Fry 3 to 4 minutes on each side or until golden brown.

William Baker
Deltona, Florida

Cheddar Cheese Fillets

2 T. milk
1 egg
1 cup crushed cheese crackers
½ cup flour
Salt, to taste
Pepper, to taste
Crappie fillets
Canola oil

In small bowl, mix milk and egg together. In separate bowl, mix crackers, flour, salt and pepper. Dip crappie fillets in milk mixture, then into cracker mix. Fry in heavy skillet with ¼ inch of canola oil until golden brown.

Allan K. Bundy
Ord, Nebraska

Ginger Striped Bass

2 to 4 lbs. striped bass fillets
1 cup peanut oil
4 T. chopped fresh garlic
4 T. minced fresh gingerroot
Soy sauce, to taste
Scallions, chopped

Steam fillets in steamer until just cooked. Place peanut oil in skillet and bring to low heat. Slowly brown garlic and ginger, being careful not to burn. Once browned, remove garlic and ginger from oil; reserve oil. Place steamed fillets in large glass baking dish; drizzle with soy sauce. Sprinkle garlic and ginger over the fillets. Heat remaining peanut oil until hot; drizzle over steamed fillets. Garnish with scallions.

Russ Franco
Yuba City, California

Grilled Panfish

Panfish fillets
¼ cup lemon juice
¼ cup olive oil
¼ cup soy sauce
1 to 2 cloves garlic, crushed

Arrange single layer of fillets in large glass baking dish. In small bowl, mix together lemon juice, olive oil, soy sauce and garlic. Pour over fillets; marinate at least 1 hour, turning once. Preheat gas grill 10 minutes. Cover grill racks with foil, spray with nonstick cooking spray. Grill fillets 4 minutes on each side or until fish flakes easily.

Janice Pauls
McPherson, Kansas

Crunchy Potato Perch

2 cups flour
Morton's Nature Seasoning
2 to 3 eggs
Instant potato buds
Perch fillets

In small bowl, mix together flour and Morton's Nature Seasoning. In another bowl, beat eggs. Place potato buds in separate bowl. Dip fillets in seasoned flour, then dip in eggs. Roll fillets in potato buds; deep fry until golden brown.

Mike Vondrak
Newport, Michigan

Ginger Striped Bass

20-Minute Fish

½ cup ketchup
4 T. butter, melted
2 tsp. lemon juice
Perch fillets
Salt, to taste
Pepper, to taste

Preheat oven to 400°F. In shallow baking pan, combine ketchup, butter and lemon juice. Arrange fish on top and sprinkle with salt and pepper. Bake for 20 minutes.

Nancy Hromada
Afton, New York

Baked Crappie

2 to 3 lbs. crappie fillets
1½ cups French dressing
2 T. lemon juice
Salt, to taste
1 (13½-oz.) can French fried onions
¼ cup grated Parmesan cheese

Place fillets in shallow baking pan. Combine dressing, lemon juice and salt. Pour sauce over fillets and let stand 30 minutes, turning once. Preheat oven to 350°F. Remove fillets from sauce; place in baking dish coated with nonstick cooking spray. In separate bowl, crush French-fried onions and add Parmesan cheese; mix well. Sprinkle mixture on fillets. Bake for 20 to 25 minutes or until fish flakes easily.

William Baker
Deltona, Florida

Baked Southwestern Bass

2 cups crushed Ritz crackers
1 carton T. Marzettis Southwestern Ranch Veggie Dip
6 bass fillets

Preheat oven to 375°F. Pour cracker crumbs into bowl. Put ⅓ of dip into separate small bowl. Dip bass in veggie dip and cover completely. Roll bass in cracker crumbs. Bake for 45 minutes or until cracker crumbs are brown.

Paul Johnson
Suwanee, Georgia

Stuffed Striped Bass

1 striped bass, butterflied, boned and opened flat with head and tail left on
1 T. lemon juice
¼ cup chopped parsley
¼ cup grated Parmesan cheese
1 cup dry bread crumbs
4 T. unsalted butter, melted
½ tsp. salt
¼ tsp. black pepper

Preheat oven to 400°F. Spray 15 x 10-inch jelly roll pan with nonstick cooking spray. Rub inside of fish with lemon juice. Place fish, skin side down, with cavity open in prepared pan. In small mixing bowl, stir together remaining ingredients. Press bread crumb mixture evenly into open cavity. Bake, uncovered, for 15 to 20 minutes or until golden.

James A. Swagel
Columbia, South Carolina

Beer-Battered Bass

2½ to 3 lb. largemouth bass
1 cup flour
¾ tsp. baking powder
¼ tsp. salt
⅛ tsp. white pepper
6 oz. dark beer
½ egg, beaten
Vegetable oil

Fillet bass and trim. Cut each fillet in half crosswise so as to have 4 portions. Sift together flour, baking powder, salt and white pepper. In separate bowl, add beer to egg and whisk together. Add beer mix to flour mix, whisking until smooth. Heat oil in skillet to 350°F. Lightly season fillets with salt and dredge in flour. Shake off excess. Dip into batter to coat. Drop into hot oil. Fry until deep golden brown and cooked through.

Henry Tardiff
Bennington, New Hampshire

Oven-Baked Bass

4 medium-sized whole bass
2 large onions, sliced
1 lemon, sliced
¼ cup butter, melted
¼ tsp. garlic powder
Salt, to taste
Pepper, to taste

Preheat oven to 400°F. Place fish in baking pan. In large bowl, combine onions, lemon, butter and garlic powder. Toss until onions are well coated. Pour over bass. Sprinkle with salt and pepper. Bake, covered, until tender.

Bob Rhoads
Mount Vernon, Indiana

Bacon-Wrapped Bass Sandwich

Bacon-Wrapped Bass Sandwich

½ lb. bacon
2 large onions, sliced
4 bass fillets
Blackening seasoning
Roll or bread
Salt, to taste
Pepper, to taste
American cheese

Line bottom of baking pan with bacon. Place layer of onions on top of bacon, then place fillets on top of onions. Lightly sprinkle fillets with blackening seasoning. Bake at 350°F for 20 to 30 minutes. Remove fillet from pan and place on roll or bread. Top with salt, pepper and slice of American cheese.

Hank Andrews
Osage Beach, Missouri

Foiled Bass Amandine

1 T. butter, softened
4 thin red onion slices
1 lemon, sliced
2 T. sliced almonds
¼ cup sliced green onions
2 (6 oz.) largemouth bass fillets,
   skinless
⅛ tsp. salt
⅛ tsp. white or lemon pepper
Paprika, to taste

Heat grill to medium-high heat. Grease center of a 20 x18-inch sheet of heavy-duty aluminum foil with butter. Arrange 2 slices each of red onion and lemon on buttered foil. Sprinkle with 1 tablespoon of almonds and half the green onions. Arrange fillets in single layer over onions, lemon and almonds. Sprinkle lightly with salt, pepper and paprika. Fold the long sides of foil together in locked folds. Fold and crimp short ends; seal tightly. Repeat with second fillet. Place packets directly on the cooking grate. Grill, covered, for 11 to 15 minutes, or until the fish is firm, opaque and just begins to flake.

Greg Haut
Waukesha, Wisconsin

Baked Cream Cheese Bluegill

1 (3-oz.) pkg. cream cheese
1 pkg. dry macaroni
1 (10-oz.) can condensed cream of
   mushroom soup
1½ cups cooked, flaked bluegill
¼ cup chopped onion
¼ cup chopped green pepper
2 T. prepared mustard
¼ tsp. salt
¼ cup milk
½ cup corn flake crumbs

Preheat oven to 375°F. Allow cream cheese to soften at room temperature. Prepare macaroni according to package directions; drain. Blend soup and cream cheese together. Stir in macaroni, fish, onion, pepper, mustard, salt and milk. Place mixture in 1½-quart baking dish. Sprinkle with corn flake crumbs. Bake for 20 to 25 minutes.

Henry R. Andrews
Osage Beach, Missouri

Trout & Salmon

Some anglers would cringe at the thought of eating a trout. These are people that never pulled a couple brookies from a crystal-clear stream, shucked out the fishes' innards, heated up a little butter in tiny black frypan, and ate the creatures, bones and fins and all, to the music of tumbling waters. Once again — restraint is key, only saving to eat what the resource can spare. Salmon's a little different: Big, brawny, often destined to die anyway at some point in the fairly near future — might as well keep the fish and eat it! And of course, it's as good as anything, all pink and full of its own unique salmon flavor.

Curried Salmon Steaks,
Page 92

83

Blackened Salmon Benedict

Blackened Salmon Benedict

Per Serving
Vinegar
1 egg
1 English muffin
¼ cup butter
1 T. lemon juice
Salt, to taste
Cracked pepper, to taste
2 egg yolks
4 to 6 oz. salmon fillet
Blackening spice, to taste

Add some vinegar to saucepan; simmer. Add egg; swirl around with fork until egg takes round form. Poach egg until egg white is solid. Drain off water. Toast English muffin.

In double boiler over low heat, add butter, lemon juice, salt and pepper. Add egg yolks, stirring until sauce is consistent. Dip salmon fillet in melted butter. Coat each side with blackening spice. Grill over medium flame until fish is flaky. Do not turn fish over until spice has made a tough skin over fish or spice will pull off.

Place English muffin on plate. Put egg on muffin and fish on top of egg. Spoon sauce over fish; garnish with cracked pepper.

Craig Henry
Montgomery, West Virginia

Overnight Baked Trout for Campers

Large trout
Salt, to taste
Pepper, to taste

Reserve larger fish for this overnight cooking. At night, clean fish; remove heads. Season inside and out with salt and pepper. Roll each fillet separately in waxed paper, folding ends in. Wrap in thick, wet newspaper. Dig trench for each fish just deep enough to allow 1 inch of earth on top. Bury fish bundles; build campfire over trenches and leave until breakfast time.

Hanne Anderson
Council, Idaho

Corn Flaked Lake Trout

½ cup flour
4 eggs
6 handfuls crushed corn flakes
Cooking oil
Trout fillets, cubed

Put flour in small bowl. In separate small bowl, beat eggs until well mixed. In third small bowl, place corn flakes. Pour enough cooking oil into skillet so that fish is almost covered. Heat oil on stove or fire over medium-high heat. Wash fish in cold water; pat dry until no excess water remains. Dip fish pieces into flour, then eggs, then corn flakes. Place dipped fish pieces into skillet. Fry one side 3 to 4 minutes or until bottom of fish turns golden brown. Turn fish over; fry until fish is golden brown on other side. Place fish into bowl lined with paper towels to absorb excess oil. Serve warm.

Ed Leerdam
Scarborough, Ontario, Canada

Warm Salmon Salad

1 lb. salmon, filleted, skinned
2 T. sesame oil
½ orange rind, grated
Juice of 1 orange
1 tsp. Dijon mustard
1 T. chopped fresh tarragon
Salt, to taste
Ground black pepper, to taste
3 T. peanut oil
4 oz. mixed salad greens
1 T. toasted sesame seeds

Cut salmon into bite-size pieces. In small bowl, combine sesame oil, orange rind, orange juice, mustard and tarragon; mix well. Season with salt and pepper. Set aside.

Heat peanut oil in skillet. Add salmon pieces; fry 3 to 4 minutes, until lightly brown, but still tender inside. Add dressing to salmon; toss together gently; heat 30 seconds. Remove from heat.

Arrange salad greens on serving plates. Spoon salmon and cooking juices over salads and garnish with toasted sesame seeds.

Greg Martin
Orlando, Florida

San Juan Trout

4 medium trout, gutted and gilled
¼ tsp. salt
Water
6 T. butter
¼ tsp. paprika
¼ tsp. ground allspice

Place trout in large skillet. Salt fish; add enough boiling water to cover fish; simmer 6 minutes. Remove trout; drain pan. In saucepan, melt butter; add paprika and allspice. Skin and bone fish; lay meat on warm platter. Pour butter sauce over fish; serve.

Rich Beaudry
Pagosa Springs, Colorado

Emeril Legasse's Creole Trout

4 to 6 trout, dressed
Butter
2½ T. paprika
2 T. salt
2 T. garlic powder
1 T. black pepper
1 T. onion powder
1 T. cayenne pepper
1 T. dried oregano
1 T. dried thyme
Salt, to taste
Pepper, to taste
1 onion, sliced

Place trout on aluminum foil. Place slices of butter inside and outside of fish. In small bowl, mix paprika, salt, garlic powder, black pepper, onion powder, cayenne pepper, oregano and thyme. Sprinkle seasoning inside and outside of trout. Add salt and pepper. Place slices of onion inside fish; wrap in aluminum foil and grill until fish flakes easily.

Chris Hastings
East Longmeadow, Massachusetts

The Water's Bounty

Salmon Croquettes

4 oz. salmon, cooked
1 cup mashed potatoes
1 egg, beaten
½ tsp. salt
Dash of pepper
¼ tsp. celery salt
1 T. butter, melted

Flake salmon with fork. In medium bowl, combine mashed potatoes, egg, salt, pepper, celery salt and butter. Add salmon; mix well. Form into balls. Drop in deep fryer for 3 minutes at 375°F. Drain on paper towels.

Joseph Amey
North Highlands, California

Grilled Salmon Even the Kids Will Eat

1 large, whole salmon
1 lemon, sliced
1 tomato, sliced
1 green pepper, slivered
Salt, to taste
Pepper, to taste

Wash fish; pat dry. Place slices of lemon inside fish, followed by tomato and green pepper. Salt and pepper lightly. Layer lemon, tomato and green pepper on top of fish; add salt and pepper. Wrap in heavy aluminum foil and bake for 1 to 1¼ hours or until fish flakes easily.

Hanne Anderson
Council, Idaho

Trout in Foil

2 to 3 medium trout
1 tsp. butter
1 tsp. lemon juice
¼ tsp. garlic powder
¼ tsp. dried parsley
Salt, to taste
Pepper, to taste
1 onion, thinly sliced
1 tomato, sliced
¼ green pepper, thinly sliced
½ cup white wine

Preheat grill to medium heat, or preheat oven to 350°F. Place fish on piece of aluminum foil, folding the foil into rectangular boats to keep fluids from dripping out. Cover fish cavity with butter. Sprinkle inside and outside of fish with lemon juice, garlic powder, parsley and salt and pepper. Lay slices of onion, tomato and pepper on top. Pour wine around fish. Seal aluminum foil, leaving space for steam to escape. Cook fish 10 minutes for each inch of thickness, or until fish flakes easily.

Randy Webb
Fife Lake, Michigan

Big Meadow Mushroomed Trout

Big Meadow Mushroomed Trout

4 medium trout, gilled and gutted
Flour, seasoned
4 T. butter
1 tsp. cooking oil
6 large mushrooms, sliced
2 T. lemon juice

Roll trout in seasoned flour. Fry in butter and oil until fish flakes easily and skin is golden brown. Sauté mushrooms in butter until tender. Add lemon juice; pour over trout.

Rich Beaudry
Pagosa Springs, Colorado

Salmon Pie

2 cups cooked rice
3 T. grated Parmesan cheese
1 egg white
1 cup cooked, flaked salmon
½ cup milk or half-and-half
3 eggs, slightly beaten
1 cup small curd cottage cheese
¼ cup chopped onion
2 T. flour
2 T. parsley
⅛ tsp. salt
⅛ tsp. pepper
⅛ tsp. ground oregano
Paprika (optional)

Preheat oven to 375°F. Spray 9-inch pie plate with nonstick cooking spray. In medium bowl, mix rice, Parmesan cheese and egg white. Press into pie plate; set aside. In separate medium bowl, combine salmon, milk, eggs, cottage cheese, onion, flour, parsley, salt, pepper and oregano. Pour mixture into crust. Sprinkle with paprika, if desired. Bake for 30 to 40 minutes, or until knife inserted into center comes out clean. Let stand 10 minutes before cutting.

Robert Gagnon
Dayton, Ohio

Brown Sugar & Bourbon Salmon with Toasted Almonds

4 (6 oz.) salmon fillets
Sweet bourbon
¼ cup water
¼ cup light brown sugar
Almonds, sliced

Marinate salmon fillets in bourbon overnight. Next day, add water to sugar; stir until thick consistency. Put almonds on cookie sheet; broil until browned. Grill salmon over medium heat until fish flakes; brush with sugar mixture often.

Craig Henry
Montgomery, West Virginia

Salmon Cheese Ball

2 (8-oz.) pkgs. cream cheese
1 stick butter
1 T. grated onion
1 T. lemon juice
1 T. horseradish
1 tsp. salt
⅛ tsp. pepper
1 cup cooked, flaked salmon
½ cup chopped pecans
1 T. chopped parsley

Mix cream cheese, butter, onion, lemon juice, horseradish, salt and pepper together. Stir in fish. Cover and refrigerate 1 to 2 hours. Roll into ball. In small bowl, mix pecans and parsley. Sprinkle mixture over fish; refrigerate 3 to 4 hours.

Robert Gagnon
Dayton, Ohio

Fish Kabobs

Bacon
1 salmon fillet, skinned and cut
1 cup ketchup
1 cup barbecue sauce
2 T. brown sugar
¼ cup lemon juice
⅛ cup teriyaki marinade
⅛ cup Worcestershire sauce
Dash of hot sauce, to taste

Wrap half strip of bacon around each 1-inch-square piece of fish. Pin with 6-inch bamboo or metal skewer. In medium bowl, mix ketchup, barbecue sauce, brown sugar, lemon juice, teriyaki, Worcestershire and hot sauce. Place skewers in flat pan; pour mix over kabobs. Refrigerate for 1 hour. Roll kabobs to thoroughly coat with marinade. Refrigerate additional hour. Barbecue or broil until bacon is slightly crispy, turning as necessary to cook all sides.

Mark Haase
Kalama, Washington

Trout in Dijonaise Mushroom Sauce

3 trout, cleaned and heads removed,
    butterfly style
2 cups flour
6 oz. butter, cubed
1 lb. mushrooms, sliced
½ bunch green onions, diced
10 oz. chicken broth
5 T. Dijon mustard
Salt, to taste
Pepper, to taste

Dredge trout in flour; cook each individual fish in large sauté pan with 2 oz. butter. Place cooked trout on baking pan; keep warm in oven. In same sauté pan, add 2 oz. butter, mushrooms and green onions. Cook over medium-high heat for 5 minutes. Add chicken broth, mustard, salt and pepper. Cook 5 to 7 minutes. Turn heat to low; add remaining 2 oz. butter. Stir until butter melts and sauce thickens slightly. Pour sauce over trout.

James Mullen
East Meredith, New York

Salmon Patties

1 can salmon, with juices
1 pkg. crackers, finely ground
1 egg
½ large onion
Salt, to taste
Pepper, to taste
Flour
Oil

In medium bowl, combine salmon, crackers, egg, onion, salt and pepper. Blend well. Shape into medium-size patties; flour each side lightly. Fry in small amount of oil until golden brown.

Don & Martha Capps
Brighton, Illinois

Fish Relleno

Trout fillets
Oil
4 eggs, beaten
2 tomatoes, chopped
1 onion, sliced
1 bell pepper, chopped
Salt, to taste
Pepper, to taste
Soy sauce (optional)

Fry fish fillets in oil; when cooked, push to side of pan. Add eggs, turning until done. Add tomatoes, onions, bell pepper, salt, pepper and soy sauce, if desired. Put fish in serving dish with eggs and vegetables on top.

Cora Coronel
Pinallas Park, Florida

Japanese-Style Sautéed Trout 'N' Vegetables

1 trout
1½ T. olive oil
1 (16-oz. pkg.) Japanese-style
   vegetables
¼ cup water
1 T. soy sauce
½ tsp. ginger

Sauté trout in olive oil until just tender. Shred trout into pieces. In separate pan, cook vegetables in water for 5 minutes. Stir soy sauce and ginger into vegetables; add shredded fish. Cook 5 to 10 minutes more. Let cool.

Jonathan Rodriguez
Twain Harte, California

Curried Salmon Steaks

1 tsp. ground ginger
1 tsp. minced garlic
1 tsp. ground turmeric
1 tsp. chili powder
2 tsp. salt
½ tsp. ground cinnamon
½ tsp. ground cardamom
½ cup plus 4 tsp. chopped onion
1 cup water
4 T. olive oil
2 bay leaves
4 dried red peppers
4 salmon steaks

In small bowl, combine ginger, garlic, turmeric, chili powder, salt, cinnamon, cardamom, 4 teaspoons chopped onion, and 1 cup of water. Heat oil. Cook ½ cup chopped onion in oil. Add contents of small bowl. Cook until onion is transparent. Add bay leaves and red peppers; stir. Cover and cook over low heat 10 minutes. Remove from heat and let cool. Put salmon steaks in shallow casserole dish. Pour cooled sauce over steaks. Marinate in refrigerator overnight. Cook steaks on barbecue grill, basting regularly with marinade.

Tom Sauder
Colorado Springs, Colorado

Stuffed Salmon

⅓ cup butter
2 medium onions
2 cups bread crumbs
1 tsp. savory
1 tsp. salt
Pinch of pepper
1 egg
7 to 8 lb. salmon
3 T. lemon juice
Vegetable oil

Preheat oven to 425°F. Melt butter in saucepan. Add onion; cook until browned. Add bread crumbs, savory, salt, pepper and egg; mix well. Wash and scale fish; remove fins. Rub lemon juice inside and outside of fish. Stuff salmon with mixture and sew closed. Place on greased pan; bake for 1 to 1½ hours. Baste occasionally with vegetable oil. Remove when fish flakes easily with fork.

Claude Squire
Eastport, Newfoundland, Canada

Lemon Butter Salmon Steaks

2 lbs. salmon steaks
½ cup butter
1 T. chopped parsley
1 T. liquid smoke
2 tsp. salt
Dash of pepper
2 T. lemon juice

Cut steaks into serving-size pieces. Combine butter, parsley, liquid smoke, salt, pepper and lemon juice. Baste fish with sauce. Place fish in well-greased hinged wire grills. Cook 4 inches from moderately hot coals for 8 minutes. Baste with sauce. Turn and cook 7 to 10 minutes longer or until fish flakes easily.

Mary Houchin
Swansea, Illinois

Curried Salmon Steaks

Lela's Smoked Salmon

1 cup pickling salt
1 cup brown sugar
⅓ cup lemon juice
1 tsp. garlic powder
4 oz. pure vanilla
2 tart apples, cored and sliced
2 large onions, sliced
1 (64-oz.) bottle all-natural apple
   juice
12 to 14 salmon fillets

In large bowl, combine salt, sugar, lemon juice, garlic powder, vanilla, apples, onions and 2 cups of juice; mix well. Put fish slabs in heavy duty zip-top doubled freezer bags. Divide brine between bags. Add more apple juice to fill bags to top so there is no air space. Marinate for 24 hours, turning every hour to distribute brine. Do not rinse. Smoke, according to smoker instructions, 4 to 5 hours. Allow to cool on paper towels. Wrap in newspaper. Store in refrigerator, or in freezer for up to 6 to 8 months.

Lela Jo Port
Battle Creek, Michigan

Parmesan Salmon

2 eggs
1 cup Italian bread crumbs
1 cup Parmesan cheese
Salmon fillets, cut into 6 oz. pieces
2 cups seasoned flour
1 stick butter

In small bowl, beat eggs until well blended. In separate bowl, mix bread crumbs and Parmesan cheese. Roll fillets in seasoned flour. Dip fish in egg and then roll in bread crumb mixture until well covered. Fry in butter over medium heat, making sure butter doesn't burn, 10 to 12 minutes on each side. Fry until golden brown.

Michael Vondrak
Newport, Michigan

Salmon Ravioli

Dough
2 eggs
⅓ cup vegetable oil
1 T. salt
4 cups flour
⅔ cup water

Topping
1 stick butter
½ cup finely chopped garlic

Filling
2 cans salmon, with juice
2 eggs
1 sleeve saltine crackers, finely
   ground
1 large onion, finely diced

Dough:
Beat eggs well; add oil. Add salt to flour and blend well. Add blended eggs and oil to flour; slowly add water. After mixing thoroughly with 2 knives or pastry blender, knead several minutes by hand. Divide dough in half. Roll out half of dough to desired thickness; set aside.

Topping:
Melt butter; add garlic until consistent.

Filling:
Preheat oven to 350°F. Combine salmon, eggs, crackers and onion in bowl; mix well. Spread salmon mixture over dough previously rolled out. Roll out remaining half of dough; place on top of salmon mixture. Pinch outside edges of dough closed with fork. Use pizza cutter; cut into small 1½ x 1½-inch squares. Pinch all sides of each ravioli closed with fork. Pace in baking dish; brush with topping mixture. Bake 20 to 25 minutes or until light golden brown.

Don & Martha Capps
Brighton, Illinois

Roasted Salmon & Vegetables

4 (½-inch-thick) salmon steaks
2 cups refrigerated potato wedges
2 small zucchini, quartered length-
    wise, cut into 2-inch pieces
1 red bell pepper, cut into 2-inch
    pieces
1 T. lemon juice
1 T. butter, melted
½ tsp. salt
¼ tsp. dried tarragon leaves
¼ tsp. pepper

Preheat oven to 425°F. Place salmon steaks in ungreased baking pan. Arrange potato wedges, zucchini and bell pepper around salmon. Brush salmon with lemon juice. Brush salmon and vegetables with butter; sprinkle with salt, tarragon and pepper. Bake for 25 to 35 minutes or until fish flakes easily and vegetables are tender.

Chad Lemak
Granger, Indiana

Sesame Rainbow Trout

6 trout, pan-dressed
¼ cup oil
2 T. lemon juice
¼ cup sesame seeds
½ tsp. salt
Dash of pepper

Clean, wash and dry fish. In small bowl, combine oil, lemon juice, sesame seeds, salt and pepper. Place fish in well-greased hinged grills. Baste fish with sauce. Cook about 4 inches from moderately hot coals for 5 to 8 minutes. Baste with sauce; turn and cook for 5 to 8 minutes longer or until fish flakes easily.

Mary Houchin
Swansea, Illinois

Baked Salmon

1 salmon steak
Salt, to taste
Pepper, to taste
¼ cup sour cream
4 thin lemon slices
1 tsp. minced parsley

Preheat oven to 350°F. Place salmon in greased dish. Sprinkle with salt and pepper. Top with sour cream and lemon slices. Sprinkle with parsley. Bake for 35 to 40 minutes.

Ryan Wilson
Cypress, Texas

Grilled Cutthroat with Peach Salsa

Grilled Cutthroat with Peach Salsa

½ cup chopped Vidalia onion
½ cup chopped red pepper
1 jalapeño pepper, finely chopped
3 T. parsley flakes
1 T. plus ¼ cup olive oil
8 peaches, peeled, pitted and
   chopped
1 cup water
½ cup sugar
¼ cup apple cider vinegar
1 tsp. salt
½ tsp. chili powder
¼ tsp. black pepper
¼ tsp. garlic powder
3 lbs. trout fillets
Onion powder, to taste
Black pepper, to taste

In large skillet, sauté onion, pepper, jalapeño and parsley in 1 tablespoon olive oil over medium heat for 5 minutes or until tender. Add peaches, water, sugar, apple cider vinegar, salt, chili powder, black pepper and garlic powder to skillet; mix well. Cook over medium heat for 30 minutes, stirring frequently. Refrigerate salsa at least 2 hours before serving. Grill trout fillets in ¼ cup olive oil. Add onion powder and black pepper. Serve peach salsa over trout.

Peter J. Carmon
Cody, Wyoming

Honey-Sugar Glazed Barbecued Salmon

1 part honey
1 part brown sugar
1 part butter
1 to 2 tsp. liquid smoke
1 tsp. lemon juice
1 salmon fillet, skin on

Place honey, brown sugar, butter, liquid smoke and lemon juice in small microwaveable bowl; heat until butter is melted. Mix well. Cut fillets into serving-size pieces. Place fish meat side down on hot, greased grill. Baste fish with sauce. Baste fish 1 to 2 more times while cooking. Cook until fish flakes easily. Remove fish by sliding spatula between fillet and skin, leaving skin on the grill.

Paul C. Rusanowski
Juneau, Alaska

Canned Salmon

Salmon steak
½ tsp. salt
½ tsp. salad oil
2 T. vinegar
1¼ tsp. ketchup
Water

Fillet salmon off backbone, ribs and skin. Cut into 2 x 2-inch chunks. Place in scalded pint jars. Add salt, salad oil, vinegar, ketchup and enough water to fill jar three quarters full. Process in pressure cooker 90 minutes at 10 pounds pressure.

Kenneth W. Finch
Minot, Maine

Robin Anderson's Steamed Trout Salad

5 rainbow trout, cleaned, skinned, deboned
⅛ cup lime juice
⅛ cup lemon juice
Cracked pepper, to taste
1 medium sweet onion, thinly sliced
1¼ tsp. garlic powder
10 fresh basil leaves
5 T. salad dressing
5 tsp. chopped celery
5 T. sweet pickle relish
Sliced grapes (optional)
Slivered almonds (optional)

Place trout on steam rack; cover with lime juice, lemon juice, pepper, onion and garlic powder. Steam, covered, 8 to 10 minutes or until fish flakes easily with fork. While fish is cooling, chop steamed onion and place in mixing bowl. Add cracked pepper and basil leaves to onions. Flake fish in bowl; add salad dressing, celery and relish. Mix lightly; chill at least 1 hour. Serve over lettuce and tomato slices. Add grapes and almonds, if desired.

Robert E. Anderson Jr.
Liberty, Missouri

Louisiana Cajun Salmon Croquettes

½ to ¾ lb. red salmon
1 yellow onion, finely chopped
1 green pepper, chopped
2 slices bread, chopped
1 medium white potato, boiled and mashed
1 large egg
1 tsp. black pepper
Cornmeal
Oil

Boil salmon until tender. Drain; let stand until cool. Combine onion, green pepper, bread, potato, egg and black pepper; mix well. Shape into patties. Coat in cornmeal and fry in oil on high heat 2 to 3 minutes, turning once. Lay on paper towels to absorb excess oil.

Albert Hill Sr.
Floydada, Texas

Chinook Chowder

3 T. butter
¼ cup chopped onion
3 T. flour
Dash of pepper
½ tsp. salt
2½ cups milk
1 bay leaf
2 cups cooked, flaked chinook
1 T. parsley
2 potatoes, peeled, cooked and cubed

In 3-quart saucepan, melt butter and sauté onion. Blend in flour, pepper, salt, milk and bay leaf. Cook and stir until thick and bubbling. Add salmon, parsley and potatoes. Heat for 15 minutes.

Ray Murley
Oshawa, Ontario, Canada

Robin Anderson's Steamed Trout Salad

Lake Trout Pancakes

1 cup pancake mix
1 cup milk
1 egg
1 T. salad oil
1 (7¾-oz.) can trout
White sauce

Combine pancake mix, milk, egg, and salad oil; stir until smooth. Drain and remove skin and bones from trout; add half of trout to batter. Heat pancake griddle or skillet, oil lightly and fry cakes until golden brown on both sides. Add remaining trout to prepared white sauce; serve over hot pancakes.

Ray Murley
Oshawa, Ontario, Canada

Trout with Sage

1 lemon, cut in half crosswise
2 (12 to 16 oz.) whole trout, cleaned
Salt, to taste
Pepper, to taste
18 fresh sage leaves
3 T. flour
1½ T. cornmeal
2 T. oil
2 T. butter

Cut one half of lemon into 4 thin slices crosswise and the other half into wedges. Rinse fish, pat dry; sprinkle inside and outside with salt and pepper. Tuck 3 sage leaves and 2 lemon slices into cavity of each fish. Mix flour and cornmeal. Roll fish in mixture to coat; shake off excess. Heat heavy skillet over medium-high heat. When skillet is hot, add oil. Add trout and brown on each side, turning once, 6 minutes on each side. Transfer fish to warm platter. Add butter and remaining sage leaves to skillet; shake skillet often until butter is melted and sage leaves are slightly brown, about 1 minute. Spoon butter and leaves over fish. Squeeze lemon wedges over fish and add salt and pepper.

Donna Weissenbrunner
Molalla, Oregon

Lela's Fish Jerky

1 cup soy sauce (or teriyaki)
4 T. Worcestershire sauce
4 T. steak sauce
2 tsp. garlic powder
2 tsp. black pepper
2 tsp. kosher salt
2 tsp. liquid smoke
1 medium onion, sliced into rings
6 to 7 lbs. trout, center bone
   removed and sliced ¼ inch thick

Mix soy sauce, Worcestershire sauce, steak sauce, garlic powder, black pepper, kosher salt, liquid smoke and onion. In heavy-duty doubled freezer bags, marinate fish slices in mixture for 24 to 48 hours, turning bag every few hours. Do not rinse. Dry fish on screen or racks in warm oven (150°F) or in a dehydrator until dry. Allow to air dry and cool on paper towels for 1 hour.

Lela Jo Port
Battle Creek, Michigan

Steelhead Chowder

1 chicken bouillon cube
1 cup boiling water
¼ cup margarine
½ cup chopped onion
¼ cup chopped green pepper
2½ cups cooked and flaked rainbow
    trout
1 (8-oz.) can whole kernel corn
1 (16-oz.) can tomatoes
½ tsp. salt
Dash of pepper
½ tsp. thyme

Dissolve bouillon cube in boiling water. In separate skillet, melt butter and cook onion and green pepper until tender. Combine trout, corn, tomatoes, salt, pepper and thyme; cool on low heat for 15 minutes to blend flavors.

Ray Murley
Oshawa, Ontario, Canada

Salmon Salad

2 lbs. salmon, cut into bite-size
    pieces, bones removed
1 raw egg yolk
2 eggs, hard boiled and mashed
Fine salad oil
Juice of 1 lemon
1 T. vinegar
1 tsp. mustard
1 tsp. sugar
Salt, to taste
Pinch of pepper

Boil salmon; arrange on glass dish in mound. Stir raw yolk into boiled eggs; add oil a few drops at a time. Add lemon juice, vinegar, mustard, sugar, salt and pepper. Dressing must be thick. Pour mixture over salad; mix slightly with wooden spoon.

Sean Cunningham
Taylor, Texas

Salmon & Onion Chowder

Salmon & Onion Chowder

3 T. butter
12 green onions, trimmed and
    chopped
1 cup chopped onion
½ cup diced shallots
1 clove garlic, minced
½ tsp. dried thyme leaves
7 cups chicken stock
1½ lbs. red potatoes, peeled and
    diced
1 cup heavy cream
Salt, to taste
Pepper, to taste
1 lb. salmon fillets, skinned and cut
    into 1-inch cubes
1 T. minced fresh chives
1 T. minced fresh parsley

In non-aluminum, heavy saucepan, melt butter. Add green onions, onions, shallots, garlic and thyme. Cover; cook on very low heat for 20 minutes. Add chicken stock and potatoes; cook on medium heat until just reaches boiling. Reduce heat to slow simmer. Add cream, salt and pepper. Partially cover; simmer 20 minutes. Add salmon; simmer 5 more minutes. Serve in bowls garnished with chives and parsley.

Donna Weissenbrunner
Molalla, Oregon

Manny's Northwest Territory Caribbean Laker Baker

1 Spanish onion, sliced
200 grams grated cheese (old ched-
    dar, Monterey Jack, etc.)
350 milliliters commercial jerk
    sauce
3 to 5 lbs. trout fillets
Salt, to taste
Pepper, to taste

On large piece of heavy-duty aluminum foil, shiny side in, put ⅓ onion, ⅓ grated cheese and ⅓ jerk sauce. Place half fillets on top of onions, cheese and sauce. Salt and pepper and place another ⅓ of onion, grated cheese and jerk sauce over the fish. Place remainder of fillets on top; put remainder of ingredients over second layer of fish. Fold foil in and make an airtight seal. Cook 10 minutes on each side over grill, or 20 minutes per side on top rack of gas grill on medium-high heat. Place package on large platter intact; cut open with sharp knife.

David Baxter
Ayton, Ontario, Canada

Catfish

Grandpa would have cringed at the sight of guys letting behemoth catfish go. But guys do it all the time these days. Grandpa probably didn't know how old that catfish was, and that it would take much of a human lifetime to grow another cat that big. We know all that today ... and also that smaller cats are the best eating anyway. What finer way to pass a summer night than sitting on the banks of a catfish river, a fire crackling beside you and a couple fishing lines in the water? Don't feel bad by saving a few catfish to eat, especially those one- to five-pounders that clean up easy and cook up the best anyway.

Campfire Grilled Catfish with Salsa,
Page 111

105

Blackened Catfish & Butter Sauce

Blackened Catfish & Butter Sauce

⅓ lb. bacon
2 tsp. garlic powder
2 tsp. thyme
2 tsp. white pepper
2 tsp. black pepper
2 tsp. cayenne pepper
2 tsp. lemon pepper
2 tsp. cumin
2 tsp. crushed rosemary
2 tsp. crushed fennel seed
1 tsp. allspice
1 tsp. oregano
½ tsp. salt
4 catfish fillets
Olive oil

Lemon Butter
¼ cup butter, melted
1 tsp. lemon juice
½ tsp. hot sauce
Green onions, sliced

In large skillet, fry bacon. Discard bacon and keep grease. In small bowl, combine garlic powder, thyme, peppers, cumin, rosemary, fennel seed, allspice, oregano and salt. Rub fillets with olive oil, then coat liberally with spice mixture. Drop fillets in hot bacon grease and cook until fish flakes easily. Drain fish on paper towels.

Lemon Butter:
In small bowl, mix together butter, lemon juice, hot sauce and onions. Pour lemon butter sauce over fillets and serve.

Henry R. Andrews
Osage Beach, Missouri

Italian Pecan-Catfish Bake

2 eggs
1 cup milk
1 cup flour
1 cup Italian seasoned bread crumbs
1 stick butter
6 catfish fillets
1 tsp. Cajun shake
½ cup Italian seasoned marinade
1 cup finely chopped pecans
1 T. lemon juice

In small bowl, combine eggs and milk. Place flour and bread crumbs in two separate bowls. Melt half stick butter in large skillet. Dip fillets in egg mixture, then in flour mixture. Dip fillets in egg mixture again, then into Italian bread crumbs. Place fillets in skillet over low heat. Sprinkle fish with Cajun shake. Preheat oven to 350°F. In medium bowl, combine remaining half stick butter, Italian marinade, pecans and lemon juice. When fish flake easily, remove from skillet and place on platter. Spread pecan mixture over fillets; bake 10 minutes, covered.

Don & Martha Capps
Brighton, Illinois

Fried Catfish Casserole

Catfish fillets
Milk
Flour
1 stick butter
1 small red or green bell pepper
Onion, sliced
2 cans shrimp soup
1 small can sliced mushrooms
Juice of 1 lemon
½ cup sherry
Salt, to taste
Pepper, to taste
2 dashes of Worcestershire sauce

Soak fish in milk 2 to 3 hours. Preheat oven to 350°F. Dip fish in flour; brown in butter in skillet. Place fish into 2-quart baking dish. Brown pepper and onion in butter until limp. Add shrimp soup, mushrooms and ½ mushroom juice, lemon juice, sherry, salt, pepper and Worcestershire. Pour over fillets and bake for 30 to 40 minutes. If cooking over campfire, soak in milk 20 minutes and cook 40 to 45 minutes.

Henry R. Andrews
Osage Beach, Missouri

Tortilla-Crusted Catfish

2 lbs. catfish fillets
¼ cup cornmeal
¼ cup coarsely chopped bread
    crumbs
½ cup crushed tortilla chips
1 T. cumin
1 T. chili powder
Salt, to taste
Pepper, to taste
½ cup vegetable oil

Soak catfish in lightly salted water for 10 minutes. In medium bowl, mix together cornmeal, bread crumbs, tortilla chips, cumin and chili powder. Drain catfish; season with salt and pepper. Dip fish in crumb mixture, pressing down firmly. Heat oil in large skillet over medium heat. Shake excess breading from fillets and cook in oil 5 minutes on each side.

Joseph Barry
Burbank, Illinois

Pistachio-Crusted Catfish Fillets

2 T. olive oil
2 cups flour
1 tsp. salt
1 tsp. pepper
8 eggs
½ cup milk
2 cups finely chopped pistachios
2 cups fine bread crumbs
4 to 6 thick catfish fillets

Preheat oven to 400°F. Heat oil in skillet. In medium bowl, season flour with salt and pepper. In large bowl, mix eggs and milk. In separate bowl, mix together pistachios and bread crumbs. Dip fillets in flour mixture, then in egg mixture. Roll fillets in pistachio mixture. Place fillets in hot oil; lightly brown both sides. Remove from skillet and place in oven. Cook 8 to 10 minutes or until fish is done.

Jeffery S. Mueller
North Sioux City, South Dakota

Catfish Fillets

4 medium catfish
1 large egg
2 T. water
2 tsp. garlic powder
1 cup cornmeal
½ tsp. salt
1 tsp. basil
½ tsp. thyme
½ tsp. cayenne pepper
4 T. canola oil

Rinse fish and pat dry. In small bowl, mix together egg and water. In large, shallow pan, mix together garlic powder, cornmeal, salt, basil, thyme and cayenne. Dip fish into egg mixture, then coat with cornmeal mixture. Heat oil in skillet. Reduce to medium heat. Fry fish approximately 5 minutes on each side, or until it flakes easily.

Bill Macdonald
Hercules, California

Gourmet Catfish

Catfish
Butter, melted
Juice from 2 lemons
Salt, to taste
Pepper, to taste
1 onion, sliced
Chives, diced
Orange

Clean catfish, but do not behead. Place fish in aluminum foil and baste with butter and lemon juice. Sprinkle with salt and pepper. Lay onion slices on top of fillets, then sprinkle with chives. Place orange peelings on top, squeezing some orange juice onto fish. Wrap fish in aluminum foil; grill 20 minutes.

Roger Sturbaum
Novi, Michigan

Fried Catfish

¼ cup milk
1 egg
1 cup flour
1 cup cornmeal
½ cup Zatarains Seasoned Fish Fry
1 to 2 tsp. Cajun/Creole seasoning
Catfish fillets
Oil

In small bowl, beat together milk and egg. In medium bowl, mix together flour, cornmeal, seasoned fish fry and Cajun seasoning. Pour oil 3 to 4 inches deep into skillet. Heat to 350°F. Dip fish in egg mixture, then into flour mix. Drop into hot oil and cook until brown. Drain on paper towel.

Donald Eads
McClure, Illinois

Campfire Grilled Catfish with Salsa

Campfire Grilled Catfish with Salsa

4 catfish fillets
½ tsp. garlic salt
½ tsp. pepper

Salsa
3 medium tomatoes, chopped
¼ cup chopped onion
2 medium jalapeño peppers,
  chopped
2 T. white wine vinegar
1 tsp. salt

Sprinkle catfish with garlic salt and pepper. Place catfish in well-oiled grill basket or grill rack. Grill on uncovered grill directly over medium-hot coals 5 minutes on each side, or until fish flakes easily.

Salsa:
In large bowl, combine tomatoes, onion, jalapeños, vinegar and salt; stir well. Let stand at room temperature 30 minutes. Serve with catfish fillets.

Henry R. Andrews
Osage Beach, Missouri

Catfish & Noodles

1 cup flour
1 T. salt
1 tsp. pepper
6 catfish fillets
¼ lb. butter
6 strips bacon
6 green olives
3 cups cooked noodles

Preheat oven to 350°F. In small plastic bag, combine flour, salt, pepper and fish fillets; shake well. Fry fillets in butter until golden. Remove; drain on paper towels. Position 1 strip bacon and 1 olive on each fillet with toothpick. Bake in oven for 15 minutes. Serve over hot cooked noodles.

Ray Murley
Oshawa, Ontario, Canada

Catfish Court-Boullion

1 cup chopped onion
¼ cup chopped bell pepper
¼ cup chopped celery
⅔ cup chopped green onion tops
4 to 6 lbs. catfish steaks
Salt, to taste
Pepper, to taste
½ cup oil
1 can tomato soup

In large bowl, mix together onion, pepper, celery and green onion tops. Season catfish steaks with salt and pepper. Line bottom of Dutch oven with oil. Alternate layers of catfish and vegetables in Dutch oven, starting with catfish. Cover and bring to boil on medium-high heat. Uncover, pour tomato soup on top of last layer; lower to medium heat. Do not fast boil because fish will break apart. Allow to cook 1 hour, partially covered.

Aristile Stelly
Lafayette, Louisiana

New Orleans "Cajun" Black Beans, Rice & Catfish Salad

New Orleans "Cajun" Black Beans, Rice & Catfish Salad

Dressing
2 tsp. olive oil
¼ cup lime juice
½ cup chopped cilantro
¼ cup chopped Italian parsley
½ cup red wine vinegar
½ cup sugar
2 T. cumin
½ tsp. red pepper flakes

Salad
12 oz. catfish, boneless, skinless
1 cup fat-free chicken broth
1 (16-oz.) can black beans, rinsed
   and drained
1 cup rice, cooked
½ cup chopped green onion
1 cup chopped red bell pepper
½ avocado, chopped

Dressing:
In large bowl, mix together olive oil, lime juice, cilantro, parsley, vinegar, sugar, cumin and red pepper flakes; set aside.

Salad:
Simmer catfish in chicken broth until cooked; cut into ½-inch pieces. Toss together beans, rice, onion, red pepper and dressing mixture. Chill at least 2 hours. Stir in avocado just before serving.

Albert Hill Sr.
Floydada, Texas

Catfish with Dijon Sauce

4 catfish fillets
3 T. butter, melted
1 tsp. Worcestershire sauce
1 tsp. lemon pepper
Sour cream
Dijon mustard

Rinse fillets and pat dry. In small bowl, combine butter, Worcestershire sauce and lemon pepper; mix. Brush both sides of fillets with butter mixture and place on heavy-duty aluminum foil. Combine sour cream and mustard. Heat over campfire until warm. Grill fish over medium-hot coals 5 to 8 minutes. Turn fillets and grill an additional 5 to 8 minutes, or until fish flakes easily. Serve 2 tablespoons of sour cream sauce over each fillet.

Henry R. Andrews
Osage Beach, Missouri

Chip Dipped Bullhead Fillet

1 cup milk
1 egg
Bullhead fillets
1 bag potato chips, finely crushed

In small bowl, combine milk and egg; stir well. Dip each fillet into milk mixture, then roll in potato chips, covering completely. Heat ¼ inch of oil in large skillet. Place fillets in skillet and cook each side until golden.

Milford Miller
Chicago, Illinois

Cajun Catfish

¼ cup butter
½ cup flour
1 cup finely chopped onions
½ cup finely chopped celery
2 garlic cloves, minced
1 can sliced tomatoes
1 tsp. salt
2 tsp. black pepper
¼ tsp. cayenne pepper
3 cups water
2 large catfish fillets
2 cups hot cooked rice

In deep skillet, cook butter and flour together over low heat to form a roux. Add onions, celery and garlic; sauté until tender. Add tomatoes, salt, peppers and water. Simmer, covered, 20 to 30 minutes. Add fillets and cook 15 to 20 minutes or until fish flakes easily. Serve over rice.

Henry R. Andrews
Osage Beach, Missouri

Catfish Stew

6 lbs. catfish fillets
1 pint milk
Pinch of sage
4 T. butter
Pinch of marjoram
4 T. onion powder
Salt, to taste
Pepper, to taste

Soak catfish in salt water for 1½ hours. Boil fish and salt water for 10 minutes. Drain water; add milk, sage, butter, marjoram, onion powder, salt and pepper. Simmer 15 minutes.

Ray Murley
Oshawa, Ontario, Canada

Catfish Balls

1-lb. dried catfish
1 cup mashed potatoes
4 large eggs, separated
1 small onion, minced
2 cloves garlic, crushed
1½ T. minced fresh parsley
1 cup fine bread crumbs
1 to 2 T. butter or oil

Soak catfish overnight in salt water. Drain fish and place in small saucepan; cover with cold water. Bring to boil over medium-high heat. Simmer over medium-low heat 15 to 20 minutes, until tender. Drain fish when cool. Remove all bones; flake fish. In large bowl, mix fish, mashed potatoes, egg yolks, onion, garlic and parsley; stir well and set aside. Sprinkle layer of bread crumbs on plate. Roll fish mixture into small balls, then roll balls in bread crumbs. Heat oil in large saucepan. Fry balls 3 to 6 minutes until golden brown. Remove from saucepan and drain on paper towels.

Albert Hill Sr.
Floydada, Texas

Campfire Catfish Stew

5 lbs. catfish, dressed
Milk
Cornmeal
Oil
½ lb. bacon, diced
3 lbs. red potatoes, diced
2 lbs. white onions, diced
4 cups water
6 eggs, hard boiled, diced
1 (4-oz.) can pimiento, drained and
    diced
1 (6-oz.) can evaporated milk
Salt, to taste
Pepper, to taste

Dip fish in milk, then in cornmeal; fry in oil until flesh flakes easily. Fry bacon until crisp; remove from skillet and set aside. Fry potatoes and onions in bacon drippings until tender. Place fish in 4 cups water in cast-iron Dutch oven. Add bacon, potatoes, onions, eggs and pimiento. Simmer 1 to 1½ hours, adding water if needed. Add evaporated milk, stirring constantly, while seasoning with salt and pepper.

Henry R. Andrews
Osage Beach, Missouri

Greek-Style Channel Catfish

¼ cup butter
1 clove garlic, minced
¼ cup thinly sliced green onion
½ tsp. dried, whole oregano
½ tsp. salt
¼ tsp. freshly ground black pepper
2 T. lemon juice
2 lbs. catfish fillets, cut into 4 pieces

Melt butter in 1-cup measuring glass in microwave. Stir in garlic and green onion. Microwave additional 30 seconds or until onion is tender. Add oregano, salt, pepper and lemon juice. Set aside.

Line 12 x 8 x 2-inch baking dish with 2 layers of paper towels. Arrange fish with thickest portion to the outside of dish, overlapping thin portions in center of dish. Cover with 2 layers paper towels. Microwave on high 8 to 10 minutes, rotating dish after 3 minutes, or until fish is opaque. Let stand, covered, 3 to 5 minutes. Transfer fish to serving platter. Pour sauce over fish and serve.

Leslie J. Richardson
San Benito, Texas

Seafood

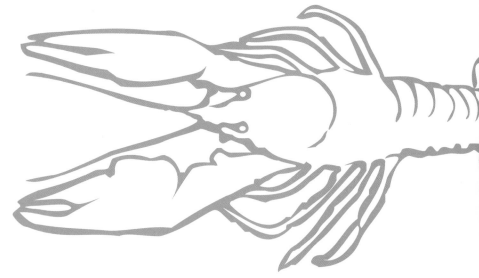

We'd be remiss if we didn't include seafood recipes—ideas for both the finned and shelled creatures of saltwater. Maybe you catch some on your own, or go out on charters, or maybe you get seafood at the market. Whatever the source, here is more fine bounty from the waters. NAFC members—from all coasts of course but from the heartland as well—contributed to this chapter, testifying to seafood's popularity and unique tastes. Tuna, flounder, shrimp, lobster, halibut, crab … it's all here and more.

Kremer Brothers' Cioppino,
Page 125

Grilled Halibut Salad

Grilled Halibut Salad

1⅓ lbs. halibut, cut into 1½-inch cubes
½ cup lemon juice
1 T. olive oil
1½ tsp. minced garlic
¼ tsp. crumbled dry mint leaves
⅛ tsp. crumbled dry oregano
1 red onion, cut into wedges
2 cups chopped fresh spinach
2 cups chopped green leaf lettuce
1 pint cherry tomatoes

Preheat charcoal grill or broiler. Rinse halibut; pat dry. In medium bowl, combine lemon juice, olive oil, garlic, mint and oregano. Add halibut chunks; stir to coat. Cover and chill 30 minutes. Drain halibut, reserving marinade. Bring marinade to boil in small saucepan; keep warm and reserve for dressing. Skewer fish, alternating red onion and halibut. Grill or broil 4 to 5 inches from heat 10 minutes or until opaque through center, turning fish once and basting with reserved marinade. In large bowl, combine spinach and lettuce. Toss in reserved dressing, tomatoes, fish and red onion. Serve.

Manuel & Karen Silva
San Jose, California

Tuna with Orange & Ginger

1 T. orange marmalade
½ tsp. peeled and finely minced gingerroot
¼ cup freshly squeezed orange juice
2 tsp. peanut oil
4 (1-lb.) tuna steaks
4 scallions, chopped

In small bowl, combine marmalade, gingerroot, orange juice and oil. Place tuna steaks in single layer in baking dish. Pour juice mixture over them. Marinate for 30 minutes. Preheat broiler or prepare grill. Reserving marinade, place tuna on broiler or grill and heat until cooked through, about 4 to 5 minutes on each side. In small saucepan or microwave safe dish, heat reserved marinade until just bubbly. Spoon over cooked tuna and sprinkle with scallions.

Leslie Richardson
San Benito, Texas

Quick Lemon-Butter Cod

1½ lbs. cod fillets
⅓ cup melted butter
2 T. flour
2 T. lemon juice
1 tsp. minced parsley

Preheat oven to 400°F. Line bottom of shallow baking pan with aluminum foil and arrange fish in single layer on top of foil. In small dish, combine melted butter, flour, lemon juice and parsley. Pour mixture over fish. Bake 15 minutes or until cod flakes easily.

Damon Black
Boise, Idaho

Sam Kernell's Grilled Tuna with Mustard

Dijon mustard
Yellowfin tuna fillet, cut into 2 x 2-
inch pieces
Garlic- and onion-flavored croutons

Put enough mustard in small dish to dip the quantity of fish you are preparing. Dip each tuna piece in mustard to lightly coat. Crush croutons in food processor; dip tuna in crumbs to cover entire piece of fish. Grill 10 minutes or until outside is brown.

Matthew Kiewiet
Altadena, California

Spicy Tuna Salad

3 eggs
2 pkgs. pesto seasoning mix
¼ cup Creole seasoning
½ cup oatmeal bran
4 albacore tuna fillets
2½ cups mayonnaise
2 tsp. lemon juice
½ red onion, chopped
1 small can diced black olives
1 small bunch fresh basil
3 T. capers, strained

Whisk eggs in large bowl, place pesto seasoning, Creole seasoning and oat bran into large zip-top bag; mix well. Place fresh albacore fillets in egg, coating all sides well. Place fillets in seasoning zip-top bag one at a time, coating well. Turn on barbecue grill to medium heat, allow 15 minutes with lid closed before placing fillets on grill. Grill fillets 8 to 10 minutes on each side. Remove fillets from grill; let cool. Once tuna is cooled, break into small chunks. Add mayonnaise, lemon juice, onion, black olives, basil and capers. Mix well with spoon, not food processor.

Karen Bolton
Carlsbad, California

Fillet of Flounder in White Wine

2 lbs. flounder fillets
½ cup white wine (Chardonnay or
　Sauvignon Blanc)
½ cup chopped onion
3 T. butter, melted
2 fresh bay leaves, crushed
1 tsp. chopped parsley
½ tsp. salt
¼ tsp. pepper

Preheat oven to 375°F. Grease shallow 2-quart casserole dish. Place fillets in dish. In large bowl, mix white wine, onion, butter, bay leaves, parsley, salt and pepper. Pour mixture over fillets. Bake for 25 minutes or until fish flakes easily when gently pierced with fork.

Leslie Richardson
San Benito, Texas

Mom's Shrimp Salad in a Spud

2 potatoes, baked
2 tsp. lemon juice
2 T. olive oil
⅛ tsp. salt
⅛ tsp. ground black pepper
1 cup cooked, shelled and coarsely
   chopped shrimp
½ cup torn or chopped lettuce
2 T. minced green onion
½ medium tomato, peeled and diced
½ small avocado, peeled and diced
2 tsp. finely chopped parsley

Cut thin slice from top of each potato. Remove pulp; dice and place in mixing bowl. Combine lemon juice, oil, salt and pepper; mix well. Set aside. Add shrimp, lettuce, green onion, tomato, avocado and parsley to diced potato; mix thoroughly. Pour lemon juice mixture over potato mixture and toss lightly. Heap mixture into potato shells.

Joseph Amey
North Highlands, California

Red Potatoes & Shrimp

6 red potatoes
Pinch of salt
Olive oil
3 cloves garlic, finely chopped
2 sprigs fresh dill, chopped
1 lb. shrimp, cleaned
1 pint tartar sauce

Place potatoes in water; add pinch of salt and boil until tender. Pour enough olive oil to cover bottom of skillet. Combine garlic, 1 sprig chopped dill and shrimp; sauté 10 minutes or until tender. Drain potatoes; split open, sprinkle remaining sprig of dill over potatoes. Add tartar sauce; spoon ingredients from skillet over tartar sauce and serve.

Jimmie Jones
San Diego, California

Baked Halibut

Oil
3 lbs. halibut
½ tsp. garlic powder
Salt
1 cup bread crumbs
2 T. parsley, chopped
2 cups water
2 to 3 T. vinegar

Preheat oven to 325°F. Rub oil over halibut. Sprinkle with garlic powder and salt. Combine bread crumbs and parsley; sprinkle over halibut. Mix water and vinegar together; pour over halibut. Bake 1½ hours or until done.

Hanne Anderson
Council, Idaho

Grilled Seasoned Halibut

1 T. Italian seasoning
1 tsp. Cajun seasoning or seasoned
    salt
1 clove garlic, minced
¼ cup butter, melted
Halibut steaks

Heat grill. Mix Italian seasoning, Cajun seasoning and garlic into melted butter. Place steaks on grill and baste until done.

David Stahlhut
Newnan, Georgia

Barbecued Clams

36 clams
4 strips lean bacon
⅓ cup ketchup
¼ lb. sharp cheese, sliced

Shuck clams and loosen from shells. Leave clams on larger half shells. Place in 2-inch-deep baking pan. Cut bacon into ½-inch pieces. Place ¼ teaspoon ketchup on each clam. Add ½-inch slice cheese. Top with bacon. Broil 5 minutes or until bacon is crisp.

Ryan Wilson
Cypress, Texas

Creamy Halibut Enchiladas

1 cup milk
1 can cream of onion or cream of
    celery soup
3 cups cooked, chunked, halibut
1 medium onion, diced
1 small can diced mild green chiles
    or jalapeños
1 small can chopped black olives
1 tomato, diced
2 cups grated Monterey Jack cheese
10 large flour tortillas

Preheat oven to 350°F. Mix milk and soup until smooth. Evenly place halibut, onion, chilies, olives, tomato and cheese over each tortilla, reserving one-third of cheese to top. Roll up tortillas and place into casserole dish. Pour soup mixture on top; sprinkle with remaining cheese. Bake for 25 minutes. Let cool 5 to 10 minutes.

Brandon Bertagnole
Park City, Utah

Creamy New England Clam Chowder

½ lb. bacon, chopped
1 cup chopped leeks
1 cup chopped yellow onions
½ cup chopped celery
1 carrot, peeled and chopped
Salt, to taste
Pepper, to taste
3 bay leaves
1 T. chopped fresh thyme
½ cup flour
1 lb. red potatoes, diced
4 cups clam juice
2 cups heavy cream
2 lbs. little neck clams, shucked and
    chopped
2 T. finely chopped parsley

In heavy Dutch oven, render bacon until crispy over medium-high heat, about 9 minutes. Stir in leeks, onions, celery and carrot. Sauté for 3 minutes or until vegetables start to wilt. Season vegetables with salt and pepper. Add bay leaves and thyme. Stir in flour; cook for 2 minutes. Add potatoes. Stir in clam juice. Bring liquid to boil and reduce to simmer. Simmer mixture 12 minutes or until potatoes are tender. Add cream; bring to simmer. Add little neck clams; simmer 2 more minutes. Stir in parsley. Season with salt and pepper, if needed.

Marc Tavares
Tiverton, Rhode Island

Camarones Enchilados Di Amore

1 lb. shrimp
¼ cup olive oil
½ onion, chopped
½ green pepper, chopped
2 cloves garlic, pressed
¼ cup chopped parsley
½ (3½-oz.) can pimientos, with
    liquid
½ (4-oz.) can tomato sauce
¼ cup ketchup
1 bay leaf
¼ cup white cooking wine
½ tsp. salt
½ tsp. freshly ground black pepper
½ tsp. Worcestershire sauce
½ tsp. hot sauce
½ T. vinegar

Clean and wash shrimp; lightly fry in hot olive oil. When shrimp are lightly pink, add onion, green pepper and garlic. Lightly fry mixture. Add parsley, pimientos and liquid, tomato sauce, ketchup, bay leaf, cooking wine, salt, black pepper, Worcestershire sauce, hot sauce and vinegar. Simmer over very low heat for 25 minutes.

Betsy & Ronney Virgillito
Pembroke Pines, Florida

Kremer Brothers' Cioppino

Kremer Brothers' Cioppino

2 lbs. clams
3 oz. extra-virgin olive oil
1 cup chopped onion
2 medium carrots, minced
1 clove garlic, minced
5 sprigs parsley, minced
1 lb. red snapper or sea bass, cut
    into 1-inch pieces
1 (2½-oz.) can crushed tomatoes
1 (14-oz.) can chicken broth
½ cup hot water, if necessary
2 bay leaves, broken
1 tsp. salt
1 tsp. Italian herbs
1 tsp. pepper
1 whole red chili
¼ cup dry white vermouth
2 whole crabs, cracked and cleaned
¾ lb. medium shrimp, raw, peeled
    with tails on
½ stick butter

Soak and scrub clams; let soak in water until ready to use. Pour oil in 6-quart saucepan. Slowly brown onion, carrots, garlic and parsley in oil. Stir in pieces of snapper. Add crushed tomatoes and cook 20 minutes. Add broth, hot water and bay leaves. Keep mixture bubbling, stirring frequently. Add salt, Italian herbs, pepper and chili. Add clams and vermouth; cook 5 minutes. Add crab and shrimp; cook additional 5 minutes. Add butter; let cook 10 additional minutes.

Gordon Kremer
Sacramento, California

Low-Fat Crab Cakes

1 lb. crab meat
½ cup bread crumbs
¼ cup low-fat mayonnaise
1 T. parsley
1 T. bay seasoning
¼ cup finely chopped scallions
¼ cup finely chopped green pepper
Hot sauce, to taste
Garlic salt, to taste

Preheat oven to 450°F. In large bowl, combine crab meat, bread crumbs, mayonnaise, parsley, bay seasoning, scallions, green pepper, hot sauce and garlic salt. Form mixture into patties and brown in saucepan coated with nonstick cooking spray. Bake for 10 to 15 minutes or until done.

David Stahlhut
Newnan, Georgia

Maddie's Deviled Clams

2 dozen clams
3 large onions
1 large bag stuffing mix
½ cup parsley flakes
2 tsp. cayenne pepper
2 tsp. black pepper
4 T. Worcestershire sauce
6 cups clam juice
Bread crumbs
Oil

Steam clams open. Put through grinder or food processor. Add onions, stuffing, parsley, red pepper, black pepper and Worcestershire sauce; mix well. Thicken clam juice with bread crumbs. Add to mixture; mix well. Roll into balls. Coat well with additional bread crumbs. Pour oil in deep fryer or skillet; fry until done.

Note: Top neck or cherrystone clams work best.

Doug Richard
Hatteras, North Carolina

Chuck's Steamer Clams

Water
Old Bay seasoning, to taste
2 lbs. mahogany clams
4 T. margarine
2 T. red wine vinegar
⅛ to ¼ tsp. hot sauce

Fill steamer pot with water; add Old Bay seasoning. Bring to boil. Clean clams and discard hulls. Steam until clams just start to open; do not overcook. In saucepan, melt margarine, vinegar and hot sauce. Remove clams from shells and add to margarine mixture.

Chuck Lincoln
Suffield, Connecticut

Clam Quiche

1 pie pastry crust
4 strips bacon
2 T. minced onion
¾ cup clam juice
¾ cup cream
4 eggs
Salt, to taste
Black pepper, to taste
Nutmeg, to taste
1 cup minced clams, drained

Line 9-inch pie plate with pastry crust; chill 3 to 4 hours. Preheat oven to 400°F. Sauté bacon until crisp; drain on paper towels. Sauté onion in bacon grease. Combine clam juice and cream. Beat eggs, combine with clam/cream liquid; add salt, pepper and nutmeg, to taste. Remove pie shell from refrigerator. Sprinkle crumbled bacon and onion on bottom; add clams. Pour custard mixture over all. Bake for 10 minutes; reduce heat to 350°F and bake until knife inserted in center comes out clean.

Doug Richard
Hatteras, North Carolina

Asian-Flavored Grilled Fish

¼ cup sesame tahini
2 T. soy sauce
2 to 3 T. honey
2 tsp. minced ginger
1½ lbs. swordfish steaks
Green onion (optional)

In small bowl, combine tahini, soy sauce, honey and ginger. Lightly oil barbecue grill; cook fish over medium-hot coals. Baste frequently with tahini sauce. Cook 3 to 4 minutes each side, until fish flakes easily. Garnish with green onion strips, if desired.

Kathleen Dadey
Oakland, California

Broiled Swordfish

2 T. butter
2 T. lemon juice
1 clove garlic, minced
4 swordfish steaks
1 tsp. dry mustard
6 flat anchovy fillets, drained and
    chopped

Turn on broiler; preheat broiler pan. In small saucepan, heat butter, lemon juice and garlic until butter is melted; set aside. Wipe fish with damp cloth. Remove broiler pan from broiler and grease well. Arrange fish in pan in single layer; baste well with garlic butter mixture; broil 4 inches from heat for 4 minutes or until lightly browned. Turn fish and sprinkle evenly with mustard and chopped anchovies. Continue broiling until fish flakes easily.

Manuel & Karen Silva
San Jose, California

Crawfish Goulash

½ cup butter
½ cup flour
1 cup chopped celery
3 toes garlic, minced
1 cup chopped green pepper
1 cup water
1 cup white wine
Green onion, to taste
4 T. chopped parsley
Old Bay seasoning, to taste
16 oz. crawfish tail meat

In large saucepan, melt butter; add flour. Stir over low fire until lightly browned. Add celery, garlic and green pepper; sauté until soft. Stir in water and white wine. Add green onion, parsley and Old Bay seasoning. Place lid on saucepan; simmer over low heat for 15 minutes. Add crawfish; simmer additional 5 minutes.

Garland Zimmerman
Malden, Missouri

Flounder with Mustard & Thyme

1 lb. flounder fillets
¼ cup oat bran
2 tsp. olive oil
½ cup chicken stock
1 tsp. Dijon mustard
½ tsp. dried thyme

Coat fillets with oat bran. Heat oil in skillet. Add fillets and sauté 3½ minutes on each side or until cooked through. Carefully remove fish to heated platter. Pour stock into skillet and whisk in mustard and thyme. Bring to boil; continue to boil until reduced by half. Pour over fish; serve hot.

Leslie Richardson
San Benito, Texas

Seafood & Pasta

Seafood & Pasta

Fish Stock
Shrimp shells and tails
1¼ cups water
3 green onions, chopped
Salt, to taste
Pepper, to taste

Pasta
Water
1 lb. pasta
2 T. olive oil

Sauce
¼ cup butter
¼ cup olive oil
8 small mushrooms, sliced
3 cloves garlic, minced
1 tsp. salt
½ tsp. pepper
1 tsp. tarragon
1½ lbs. shrimp, cooked, peeled and
   deveined
¾ cup sour cream
1 T. cornstarch
Parmesan cheese, freshly grated

Fish Stock:
Remove tails from shrimp; put tails and shells in small saucepan and add 1¼ cups water. Add onion, salt and pepper, to taste; simmer. This can be used as fish stock.

Pasta:
In separate saucepan, boil water for pasta. Cook pasta, toss with 2 tablespoons olive oil; set aside.

Sauce:
Over medium heat, melt butter and ¼ cup olive oil. Add mushrooms and garlic. Season with salt, pepper and tarragon. Stir until mushrooms are soft. Add shrimp; sauté slightly and add 1 cup broth. Heat to simmer; add sour cream. Thicken, if desired, with cornstarch. Pour over cooked pasta and serve with freshly grated Parmesan cheese.

Note: 1 cup clam juice may be substituted for 1 cup fish stock.

Kim Pendleton
Naples, Florida

Vegetable-Stuffed Flounder Rolls

10 oz. broccoli, chopped
½ cup shredded carrots
¼ cup chopped green onion
¼ cup chopped green pepper
¼ cup chopped celery
1 clove garlic, minced
1½ tsp. steak sauce
¼ tsp. ground ginger
½ tsp. chicken-flavored bouillon
   granules
⅛ tsp. freshly ground pepper
2 T. lemon juice
8 (4 oz.) flounder fillets
Paprika

Preheat oven to 350°F. Place skillet over medium heat until hot. Spray skillet with nonstick cooking spray. Sauté broccoli, carrots, green onion, green pepper, celery and garlic until vegetables are tender; stir in steak sauce, ginger, bouillon, pepper and 1 tablespoon lemon juice. Spoon one-eighth of vegetable mixture over each fillet. Spray 12 x 8 x 2-inch baking dish with nonstick cooking spray; carefully roll up fillets and place seam side down in dish. Brush with remaining 1 tablespoon lemon juice and sprinkle with paprika. Bake, uncovered, 20 to 25 minutes or until fish flakes easily.

Leslie Richardson
San Benito, Texas

Jodi's Prawn & Crab Casserole

2 cans cream of chicken soup
Seasoned salt, to taste
Pepper, to taste
Dill, to taste
Garlic, to taste
Onion powder, to taste
3 cups cooked rice
1 lb. bacon, crumbled
1 lb. prawns, cooked
1 can fresh crab meat
2 cups frozen Japanese vegetables
1 cup grated colby cheese
1 cup grated marble cheese

Preheat oven to 350°F. In large mixing bowl, combine cream soup, salt, pepper, dill, garlic and onion powder. In bottom of casserole dish, spread one layer of rice. Sprinkle layer of crumbled bacon over rice. Place some prawns and crab over bacon and rice. Spread some vegetables over prawns and crab. Pour some cream mixture over top vegetables; sprinkle with grated cheese. Repeat until all ingredients are used. Bake for 30 minutes or bake in microwave on high for10 minutes, turn, and bake additional 5 minutes.

Jodi & Robert Stubbs
Garibaldi Highlands, British Columbia, Canada

Halibut in Coconut Sauce

2 lb. halibut
1 egg
Milk
Italian bread crumbs
1 to 2 sticks butter
1 white onion, sliced
1 red onion, sliced
1 can coconut milk
Fresh tomato, cut into wedges

Cut fish into 4-ounce pieces. Mix egg and milk to make dip for fish. Dip fish in egg mix and roll in bread crumbs. Melt butter in skillet over medium heat; sauté onions until translucent. Remove onions, add pieces of fish and brown on both sides, but do not completely cook. Remove partially cooked halibut. Add more butter if needed. Put onions back into pan; add coconut milk to onions and cook, stirring frequently, until sauce thickens. Add tomato wedges and return halibut to mixture. Coat fish with sauce and cook until fish is done. Arrange fish pieces on platter and smother with onions, tomatoes and sauce.

Paul Rusanowski
Juneau, Alaska

Barbecued Shrimp

1 lb. butter
1 lb. margarine
6 oz. Worcestershire sauce
8 T. finely ground black pepper
1 tsp. ground rosemary
4 lemons, sliced
1 tsp. hot sauce
4 tsp. salt
2 to 4 cloves garlic (optional)
8 to 10 lbs. jumbo shrimp

In saucepan, melt butter and margarine. Add Worcestershire, pepper, rosemary, lemon slices, hot sauce, salt and garlic; mix thoroughly. Divide shrimp between two large shallow pans and pour heated sauce over each; stir well. Cook 15 to 20 minutes, turning once, or until shells turn pink and meat is white.

Douglas M. West
Baldwinsville, New York

Filleted Rockfish

2 lb. rockfish, filleted
Onion ring batter (or your favorite
    beer batter)
Oil
16 (6 to 8-inch) soft corn tortillas
Ensalada sauce (see recipe below)
Salsa fresca (see recipe below)
½ head green cabbage, shredded
Fresh sprigs of cilantro (optional)

Salsa Fresca
4 large tomatoes, chopped
1 large white onion, diced
2 pickled jalapeños, diced
2 T. chopped cilantro

Ensalada Sauce
¾ cup ranch dressing
½ cup sour cream
1 tsp. hot sauce
Milk

Cut fish into 1 x 4-inch strips. Prepare batter according to directions on package. Heat oil for deep frying. Heat corn tortillas on flat heated skillet and set aside; keep warm. Dip fish strips in batter; cook until golden brown. Place several strips of cooked fish lengthwise across center of warm tortilla. Top with ensalada sauce, salsa fresca, cabbage and cilantro. Great by themselves or even better with a generous portion of refried beans and Mexican rice!

Salsa Fresca:
Mix all salsa ingredients together; chill.

Ensalada Sauce:
Mix ranch dressing, sour cream and hot sauce together. Slowly add milk to thin mixture to desired consistency. It should be just pourable.

Ted Winter
Imperial Beach, California

Essentials

Man (and woman) does not live by fish alone. It's important to have a whole repertoire of salads, sauces, side dishes, appetizers and marinades to choose from, when planning and rounding out any meal. Here are ideas for all that and more—ready to accent or accompany any great fish you cook.

Cashew Fish,
Page 149

133

Salmon Salad with Avocado

Salmon Salad with Avocado

1 small shallot, peeled and chopped
1 jalapeño pepper, cored, seeded
   and minced
4 oz. smoked salmon
6 cherry tomatoes
1 T. minced, fresh cilantro
¼ tsp. pepper
2 T. lemon juice
1 small avocado, halved and pitted

In large bowl mix shallot, jalapeño, salmon, tomatoes, cilantro, pepper and lemon juice. Stir gently, but mix well. Spoon half of mixture in each avocado half.

Donna Weissenbrunner
Molalla, Oregon

Killer Pacific Northwest Salmon Barbecue Sauce

1 (64-oz.) can tomato juice
1 lb. butter
2 medium onions, chopped
2 T. minced garlic
3 bay leaves
1 tsp. black pepper
1 tsp. dill
½ tsp. crushed red pepper flakes
3 tsp. liquid smoke
½ cup soy sauce
¼ cup Worcestershire sauce
⅓ cup white vinegar

In large saucepan, mix all ingredients. Bring to boil over medium heat; lower to simmer for 1 hour. Serve with salmon.

Kent Waner
Enumclaw, Washington

Smoked Catfish Dip

¾ lb. smoked catfish
1 (8-oz.) pkg. light cream cheese,
   softened
2 T. lemon juice
¼ tsp. garlic powder
2 T. milk

In large bowl, flake fish. Combine with cream cheese, lemon juice, garlic powder and milk; mix well. Place in serving dish. Serve with crackers.

Steve Daniels
Richmond, Missouri

Pineapple Salsa

1 fresh pineapple, peeled, cored, finely diced
1 red bell pepper, finely diced
1 green bell pepper, finely diced
¼ cup chopped cilantro
¾ cup chopped basil
¼ cup chopped mint
1 T. minced, fresh ginger
1 T. cumin
1 T. curry
1 oz. lime or lemon juice
2 oz. orange juice
1 medium jalapeño, finely chopped
Salt, to taste
Pepper, to taste

Mix all ingredients well. Top grilled salmon or bass with salsa.

Karl Ulmer
Hawley, Pennsylvania

Low-Fat Fish Fry

1 egg white
⅓ cup dried bread crumbs
2 T. grated Parmesan cheese
¾ tsp. dried basil leaves
¼ tsp. pepper
½ tsp. salt
½ cup nonfat mayonnaise
2 tsp. lemon juice
1½ tsp. hot pepper sauce

Preheat oven to 450°F. In pie plate, beat egg white slightly. On waxed paper, mix bread crumbs, Parmesan cheese, basil, pepper and salt. When ready to cook fish, dip in egg white and then roll in bread crumb mixture. Coat thoroughly. Place fillets on ungreased cookie sheet. Bake for 10 to 12 minutes without turning, or until fish flakes easily. Mix together mayonnaise, lemon juice and hot pepper sauce for fat-free tartar sauce.

Elmer Spitze
Lincoln, Illinois

Tartar Sauce

¼ cup sweet pickle relish
¼ cup mayonnaise
¼ cup sour cream
1 tsp. lemon juice
1 tsp. sugar
½ tsp. onion powder
½ tsp. cider vinegar

In large bowl, combine all ingredients; whisk together and blend well. Chill. Serve with fish.

Henry L. Tardiff
Bennington, New Hampshire

Pineapple Salsa

Potato Flake Fillets

2 to 3 eggs
6 medium fillets
2 cups instant potato flakes
Butter

In small bowl, beat eggs thoroughly. When ready to prepare fish, dip fillets in eggs, then roll in potato flakes. Fry in butter, turning once, until batter browns or until fish flakes easily.

David Duncan
Alturas, California

Bluegill Dip

1 lb. bluegill fillets, cooked, flaked
1 cup sour cream
¼ cup nut dust (crush nuts in blender)
1 T. fresh lemon juice
3 T. minced onion
¼ tsp. salt

In large bowl, combine all ingredients; mix well. Chill. Serve with crackers.

Henry R. Andrews
Osage Beach, Missouri

Tempura Batter for Fish & Onion Rings

¾ cup sifted flour
¼ cup cornstarch
½ tsp. baking powder
1 cup beer or water
1 egg

Mix flour, cornstarch, baking powder, beer and egg into a batter. When ready to prepare fish, dip fillets in mixture, then pan-fry in oil. When ready to prepare onion rings, dip, drain and drop one at a time into 395°F oil.

Kenneth Finch
Minot, Maine

Magic Batter

1 cup Friers Magic
1 cup flour
1 tsp. black pepper
1 tsp. garlic powder
1 tsp. onion powder
1 T. seasoned salt

Put Friers Magic, flour, pepper, garlic powder, onion powder and salt in zip-top bag; mix well. When ready to prepare fish, place fillet in bag and coat completely. Deep fry until golden brown.

Lawrence Painter
Lawrenceville, Illinois

Cajun Seasoning Blend

6 T. paprika
2 T. black pepper
2 T. white pepper
2 T. garlic powder
1 tsp. basil
1 tsp. thyme
1 tsp. cayenne pepper
1 tsp. dry mustard
2 T. onion powder
2 T. sugar
1½ T. salt

Place all ingredients in zip-top bag and shake to blend completely. Store in shaker.

Henry L. Tardiff
Bennington, New Hampshire

Red Dipping Sauce

1½ cups ketchup
2 T. brown sugar
2 T. Worcestershire sauce
1 tsp. dry mustard
⅓ cup whiskey

In small saucepan, mix ketchup, brown sugar, Worcestershire sauce and mustard. Bring to a boil, stirring occasionally. Stir in whiskey; simmer 5 minutes. Refrigerate before serving. Serve with favorite fish.

John P. Pelrine
Chicago, Illinois

Uncle Don's Fish Dip

4 cups trout, salmon or steelhead,
   cooked, boned and chopped
½ cup finely chopped onion
½ cup finely chopped celery
¼ cup finely chopped sweet pickle
4 cloves garlic, minced
Seasoned salt, to taste
Hot sauce, to taste
1 cup mayonnaise

In large bowl, combine all ingredients; mix well. Chill. Serve with crackers, toast or bread.

Jim Fain
Susanville, California

Trout Spread

6 oz. trout, cooked and deboned
1 T. minced green onion
3 T. mayonnaise
1 tsp. lemon juice
1 tsp. lemon pepper
½ tsp. salt

In small bowl, mix all ingredients well with a fork. Refrigerate at least 2 hours before serving. Serve on crackers, bread or toast.

Jennifer Ann Kunze
Grand Rapids, Minnesota

Béarnaise Sauce

3½ T. lemon juice
2 egg yolks
½ cup butter
2 T. chopped parsley
½ tsp. tarragon
1 T. tarragon vinegar

In saucepan, stir lemon juice and egg yolks. Add half the butter; stir over low heat. Once butter is melted, add remainder of butter. Make sure butter melts slowly so eggs cook and sauce thickens without curdling. Add parsley, tarragon and tarragon vinegar.

Ray Murley
Oshawa, Ontario, Canada

Uncle Don's Fish Dip
Trout Spread

Cure for Smoking

1 qt. water
¼ cup white or brown sugar cure
¼ cup brown sugar
¼ tsp. ground pepper
3 toes garlic, finely chopped
1 tsp. soy sauce
2 tsp. Worcestershire sauce
2 tsp. liquid smoke

In large saucepan, mix all ingredients together; bring to boil. Cover fish with brine and let soak 3 days.

Steve Koester
Scales Mound, Illinois

Dill Sauce

2 hard boiled egg yolks
2 raw egg yolks
1 cup salad oil
1½ T. vinegar
¼ tsp. Worcestershire sauce
1 T. dry mustard
½ tsp. salt
¼ tsp. pepper
½ cup whipping cream
1 tsp. dill seed

Squeeze hard-boiled egg yolks through sieve. Mix with uncooked yolks and beat slowly into salad oil. Add vinegar slowly, to avoid curdling. In separate bowl, combine Worcestershire sauce, mustard, salt and pepper; add to salad oil mixture. Fold in whipping cream and dill seed just before serving.

Ray Murley
Oshawa, Ontario, Canada

Bannock Mix

1 cup flour
1 tsp. baking powder
¼ tsp. salt
¼ cup dry milk powder
1 T. shortening

Sift flour, baking powder, salt and dry milk together. Fold into shortening until whole mixture is granular.

John P. Pelrine
Chicago, Illinois

The Crowd Pleaser

1 cup Italian bread crumbs
1 cup grated Parmesan cheese
½ cup plus additional flour
Dash of Old Bay seasoning
Dash of lemon pepper
1 egg
1 cup milk
Flour

In medium bowl, mix bread crumbs, Parmesan cheese, 1 cup flour, Old Bay seasoning and lemon pepper. In smaller bowl, mix egg and milk. Prepare separate bowl of additional flour. When ready to prepare fish, lightly cover fillets with flour, dip in milk mixture, then roll in bread crumb mixture.

Jeff Skonieczny
Twinsburg, Ohio

Cucumber Sauce

1 cucumber, peeled, seeded and
    finely grated
½ cup chili sauce
1 tsp. onion juice
2 T. lemon juice
Dash of pepper
2 drops hot sauce

In medium bowl, combine all ingredients. Chill. Serve with favorite fish.

Donna Weissenbrunner
Molalla, Oregon

Best Beer-Batter Recipe

1⅓ cups flour
1 tsp. salt
¼ tsp. pepper
1 T. butter, melted
2 egg yolks, beaten
¾ cup flat beer

In medium bowl, mix together flour, salt, pepper, butter, egg yolks and beer. Stir constantly; cover and refrigerate 3 to 12 hours.

Eric Johannesen
Livingston, Wisconsin

Shore Lunch Fish Batter

½ cup milk
2 eggs
1 tsp. vinegar
¼ tsp. onion salt
¼ tsp. seasoned salt
½ cup crushed corn flakes
½ cup Bisquick
1 T. cornmeal

In medium bowl, thoroughly mix milk, eggs, vinegar, onion salt and seasoned salt. Put corn flakes, Bisquick and cornmeal in sealable container; shake. When ready to fry fish, dip fillets in milk mixture and roll in dry mixture.

Martin Sahagian
South Milwaukee, Wisconsin

Marinade for Swordfish, Shark or Tuna Steaks

¼ cup Worcestershire sauce
¼ cup dry white wine or cooking sherry
10 drops hot sauce

Mix all ingredients together; marinate fish at least 2 hours, preferably overnight.

David Stahlhut
Newnan, Georgia

Sweet & Sour Fish Sauce

½ cup vinegar
1½ T. cornstarch
1 cube beef bouillon
½ cup boiling water
⅔ cup ketchup
⅛ tsp. garlic powder
½ cup sugar

In small bowl, slowly mix vinegar and cornstarch until smooth. Dissolve beef cube in boiling water; add vinegar/cornstarch, ketchup, garlic powder and sugar. Cook 10 minutes over medium heat, stirring constantly, until thick and smooth. Serve with fish.

Ray Murley
Oshawa, Ontario, Canada

Shore Lunch Fish Batter

White & Black Bean Amandine

1 cup black beans
1 cup white beans
2 cups white rice
2 T. fresh dill
2 T. sliced almonds

Boil the black and white beans for 45 minutes to 1 hour, or until they are done. Strain. Boil rice until done. Add beans to rice; continue cooking. Add fresh dill. Add almonds when rice/bean mixture is removed from stove.

Douglas Kerr
Waynesburg, Pennsylvania

Benny's Beer Batter

2 egg whites
1½ cups Bisquick
Pinch of salt
1½ cups light beer
10 to 15 saltine crackers
8 walleye fillets

Whip egg whites to a cream. In medium bowl, mix Bisquick, salt and beer together. Stir in egg whites. Crumble crackers into separate bowl. When ready to prepare fish, dip fillets in egg mixture. Coat with crackers thoroughly; fry 2 to 3 minutes or until brown.

Benny McLean
Argyle, Minnesota

Horseradish-Sour Cream Sauce

1½ tsp. Dijon mustard
¾ cup sour cream or yogurt
2 T. freshly grated horseradish, or 1
   T. prepared horseradish
½ tsp. salt
2 T. chopped fresh dill
¼ cup milk

In medium bowl, combine all ingredients; mix well. Serve with fish.

John P. Pelrine
Chicago, Illinois

Fisherman's Favorite Barbecue Sauce

1 cup chili sauce
¼ cup olive oil
1 tsp. paprika
⅛ tsp. black pepper
2 T. Worcestershire sauce
½ cup water
½ cup lemon juice
¼ tsp. cayenne pepper
2 T. grated onion
1 tsp. sugar

In saucepan, combine all ingredients; simmer over medium heat for 15 minutes.

John P. Pelrine
Chicago, Illinois

"Tangy" Potato Salad

1 cup mayonnaise
2 T. vinegar
1½ tsp. salt
¼ tsp. pepper
1 tsp. sugar
2 T. mustard
4 cups cubed, cooked potatoes
1 cup diced celery
½ cup diced onion

Combine mayonnaise, vinegar, salt, pepper, sugar and mustard. Add potatoes, celery and onion. Cover; chill. This has a nice tangy flavor that goes great with any fish dinner or shore lunch.

Leonard Swendsen
Honesdale, Pennsylvania

Baked Onion

1 large Vidalia, Walla Walla, or
   other sweet onion
1 pat butter or margarine
¼ tsp. beef or chicken boullion
Chives or other herbs

Peel onion; cut off top and bottom to make flat. Place onion on sheet of aluminum foil. Place butter and boullion over top of onion. Chives or other herbs may be added if desired. Wrap foil around onion; place on baking sheet in 350°F oven. Cook about 45 minutes.

Allan Sly
Spooner, Wisconsin

Cashew Fish

Cashew Fish

1½ cups chopped cashews
2 T. cracked pepper
1 tsp. garlic powder
1 can evaporated milk

In small bowl, combine cashews, pepper and garlic powder. Coat fish in milk and dredge in cashew mixture.

Lela Jo Port
Battle Creek, Missouri

Spicy Creamed Corn

2 cans creamed corn
¼ tsp. nutmeg
2 tsp. sugar
3 to 4 jalapeños, chopped, seeds
   removed
Salt, to taste
Pepper, to taste
Cayenne pepper or hot sauce, to
   taste

Mix all ingredients together. In separate bowl, heat ingredients; serve. This is a perfect companion to fish.

Bob Kinzie
Bethesda, Maryland

Very Cheesy Macaroni & Cheese

3 to 4 cups macaroni
Water
Salt, to taste
Pepper, to taste
½ stick butter, cut into chunks
1 to 2 cups grated cheese (or more,
   depending on taste)
1 cup milk
1 egg, beaten

Preheat oven to 350°F. Place macaroni in large saucepan of water; add pinch of salt. Boil until tender; drain. In 2-inch casserole dish, layer macaroni. Add salt, pepper and chunks of butter. Add layer of grated cheese over macaroni. Continue layering in same alternating pattern, ending with cheese on top. In separate bowl, mix milk, egg, salt and pepper together. Pour over macaroni and cheese. Place in oven and bake until cheese has melted and milk mixture is cooked.

Albert Hill Sr.
Floydada, Texas

Cornbread with Jalapeños

3 T. cooking oil
2 cups self-rising white or yellow
    cornmeal
½ tsp. salt
1 T. sugar
1½ cups milk
2 eggs, room temperature and light-
    ly beaten
6 (or more) jalapeños, fresh or pick-
    led, seeded and chopped

Preheat oven to 400°F. Pour oil into cast-iron skillet or cornstick mold; place in oven. Mix cornmeal, salt and sugar. Combine with milk, eggs and jalapeños. Pour batter into hot pan; bake for 20 minutes.

Bob Kinzie
Bethesda, Maryland

Perfect Coleslaw

1 lb. green cabbage
6 oz. red cabbage
2 carrots
1 cup mayonnaise
½ cup sour cream
2 T. sugar
¼ tsp. salt
Dash of white pepper
1 tsp. minced garlic cloves
¼ tsp. ground celery seed
2 T. cider vinegar

Slice cabbage into thin slices. Cut into 2-inch lengths. Peel and trim carrots. Using peeler, shave carrots into thin strips. Stack strips; cut to length of cabbage, then cut into thin spears. Combine with cabbage; toss to blend. Prepare dressing by whisking together mayonnaise and sour cream. Add sugar, salt, white pepper, garlic and ground celery seed. Whisk again. Add cider vinegar; whisk again until smooth. Add dressing to cabbage, tossing until coated. Refrigerate. Serve cold.

Henry Tardiff
Bennington, New Hampshire

Fried Cabbage

1 large head cabbage
Salt, to taste
Pepper, to taste
6 strips bacon
1 T. butter

Remove cabbage core; shred cabbage. Place cabbage in large saucepan of water; boil. Add pinch of salt and pepper. Drain cabbage. In skillet, fry bacon. Crumble on paper towels. With leftover bacon drippings, fry cabbage. Add butter and bacon to cabbage and simmer for 5 to 10 minutes.

Albert Hill Sr.
Floydada, Texas

Cornbread with Jalapeños
Perfect Coleslaw

Hearty Stuffed Peppers

10 small to medium green peppers
1 medium onion, minced
3 T. cooking oil
½ lb. ground beef
½ lb. ground pork
½ cup rice (washed 10 to 15 minutes)
1 tsp. salt
1 tsp. pepper
1 large egg, beaten
2 small cans tomato sauce

Wash green peppers, cut off tops, remove and scrape seeds out with spoon. Brown onion in oil. Pour into bowl. Add meat, rice, salt, pepper and egg. Mix well. Fill each green pepper with mixture. Place peppers into deep saucepan. Pour tomato sauce on top and enough water to cover peppers. Simmer for 1-1½ hours or until rice is tender.

Albert Hill Sr.
Floydada, Texas

Seasoned Red Potatoes in Foil

6 to 8 red potatoes
2 oz. butter
1 tsp. chopped dill weed
1 tsp. minced or granulated fresh
   garlic
1 tsp. salt
½ tsp. black pepper
2 tsp. chopped parsley
½ tsp. chopped chives

Wash and lightly scrub potatoes. Cut into eighths; place on aluminum foil. Cut butter into small pieces; place over potatoes. Sprinkle with rest of seasonings and wrap tightly in foil. Grill or bake at 425°F for 15 to 20 minutes. Press on foil to test for doneness. Remove when soft; serve.

Henry Tardiff
Bennington, New Hampshire

Steelheader's Tartar Sauce

2 cups mayonnaise
1 medium onion, chopped
1 tsp. prepared mustard
3 T. chopped olives
4 T. sweet relish
2 T. chopped parsley
1 tsp. chopped chives

In large bowl, combine all ingredients; mix well. Serve with fish.

Ray Murley
Oshawa, Ontario, Canada

Potato Salad

6 medium potatoes
Water
1¼ tsp. sugar
1¼ tsp. vinegar
½ cup finely chopped onion
¾ cup sliced celery
½ cup chopped sweet pickles
1 tsp. salt
1½ tsp. celery seed
¾ cup mayonnaise
2 hard-cooked eggs, sliced

Place potatoes in saucepan; entirely cover potatoes with water. Cover; boil for 25 minutes or until almost tender. Drain well; peel warm potatoes. Quarter and slice potatoes; transfer to mixing bowl. Sprinkle potatoes with sugar and vinegar. Add onion, celery, sweet pickles, salt and celery seed to potatoes; stir mixture to combine. Add mayonnaise; fold into potato mixture. Carefully fold in sliced eggs. Cover and chill thoroughly.

William Baker
Deltona, Florida

Creamy Coleslaw

1 medium head cabbage, shredded
1 carrot, chopped
1 small onion, chopped
¾ cup salad dressing
¼ cup Italian dressing
½ tsp celery seed
¼ tsp. salt
⅛ tsp. pepper
¼ cup sugar

Mix cabbage, carrot and onion. In small bowl, combine salad dressing, Italian dressing, celery seed, salt, pepper and sugar. Add to cabbage mixture; stir. Store in covered container.

Donald Eads
McClure, Illinois

Fisherman's Beer Batter

1 cup plus 3 to 4 T. Bisquick
½ tsp. salt
1 egg
½ cup beer
Soy sauce or vinegar (optional)
1 lb. fish fillets

In medium bowl, mix 1 cup Bisquick, salt, egg and beer together. Soy sauce or vinegar can be added, if desired. When ready to prepare fish, lightly coat fillet with 3 to 4 tablespoons Bisquick. Dip fish into batter mixture; cook until golden brown.

Jane Hunter
Bullhead City, Arizona

Black Bean &
Corn Salsa Fritters

Black Bean & Corn Salsa Fritters

1 cup cornmeal
1 cup seasoned flour
2 eggs
¼ cup beer
Oil
½ cup milk
2 cups black bean and corn salsa
1 cup grated cheese (colby jack or
    cheddar)

Heat oil in cast-iron skillet. Mix dry ingredients. Beat eggs and beer together. Add to dry ingredients; mix well. Add up to ½ cup milk, in order to make consistency of pancake batter. Add salsa and grated cheese. Thin with milk if necessary. Drop by tablespoon into hot oil; cook until brown. Turn if necessary. Remove to paper bag or wire rack to drain. You can add fish or meat pieces to batter, and fritters make a complete meal.

Kim Pendleton
Naples, Florida

Classic Baked Beans

2 (16-oz.) cans pork and beans in
    tomato sauce
½ cup finely chopped onion
⅓ cup ketchup
2 T. packed brown sugar
1 T. prepared mustard
4 slices bacon, cut in half and par-
    tially cooked

Preheat oven to 350°F. In 1¼-quart ovenproof dish, combine beans, onion, ketchup, brown sugar and mustard. Top with bacon. Bake uncovered for 1 hour or until hot and bubbly. Stir before serving. Makes 6 to 8 servings.

William Baker
Deltona, Florida

Doctored Shore Lunch Beans

1 can pork and beans
1 can red kidney beans, drained
1 can mushrooms pieces, drained
3 to 5 drops liquid smoke
10 drops hot sauce
¼ cup diced onions

Place all ingredients in saucepan; combine. Simmer for 30 minutes. Stir often.

David Baxter
Ayton, Ontario, Canada

Index

The Water's Bounty